"How I wish I'd had this book forty years ago when I decided to become a writer! Reeves not only provides the creative inspiration to get us writing and keep us going, she suggests exactly the right themes and daily writings to tease out the spiritual gifts of our own creative voices. If you love writing, you've got to have this book in your library."

— **Hal Zina Bennett,** author of *Write from the Heart* and twenty-five books of nonfiction and fiction

"Hats off to Judy Reeves for this practical compendium for the budding writer. Writers have long known that daily practice is what it takes, and Ms. Reeves gives us a helping hand with daily writing exercises, useful inspirations, and pertinent quotes from Mick Jagger to Willa Cather. This Book of Days is not for the shelf but for the backpack, the desk, the bedside table. A portable feast."

— **Dorianne Laux,** professor of creative writing, University of Oregon, and coauthor of *The Poet's Companion: A Guide to the Pleasures of Writing Poetry*

"How marvelous when a creative stream pours through the psyche and we are there to write the words! Judy Reeves knows how fragile these moments are, how susceptible to our lack of courage, to enticements, to chores. *A Writer's Book of Days* counters those evils with a detailed practice: an exercise, encouraging suggestions, and quotes from working writers *for every day of the year.* Fine help for developing those precious moments when the words do flow. . . ."

— **Clive Matson,** poet, author of *Let the Crazy Child Write!*

# A *Writer's* Book of Days

# A Writer's Book of Days

A Spirited Companion and Lively Muse
for the Writing Life

Judy Reeves

NEW WORLD LIBRARY
NOVATO, CALIFORNIA

New World Library
14 Pamaron Way
Novato, California 94949

Copyright © 1999 by Judy Reeves
Edited by Gina Misiroglu
Cover design by Mary Ann Casler
Interior design and layout by Doris Doi

Jack Kerouac, "Belief & Technique for Modern Prose — List of Essentials." Reprinted by permission of Sterling Lord Literstic, Inc. ©1977 by Jack Kerouac.

Brenda Ueland, *If You Want to Write.* Excerpt from chapter XVIII, ©1987 by the Estate of Brenda Ueland. Reprinted from *If You Want to Write: A Book about Art, Independence and Spirit* with the permission of Graywolf Press, Saint Paul, Minnesota.

Scott Russell Sanders, "The Most Human Art," is excerpted from "The Power of Stories," which was originally published by *The Georgia Review.* ©1997 by Scott Russell Sanders. Reprinted by permission of the author.

Henry Miller, *Commandments,* from *Henry Miller on Writing.* ©1964 by Henry Miller. Reprinted by permission of New Directions Publishing Corp.

### Library of Congress Cataloging-in-Publication Data

Reeves, Judith, 1942-
    A writer's book of days: a spirited companion and lively muse for the writing life / written by Judith Reeves.
        p.    cm.
    Includes bibliographical references.
    ISBN 1-57731-100-0 (alk. paper)
    1. Authorship Miscellanea. 2. Creative writing Miscellanea.
I. Title
PN165.R44 1999
808.02—dc21
                                                     99-31110
                                                      CIP

First Printing, September 1999
ISBN 1-57731-100-0
Printed in Canada on acid-free paper
Distributed to the trade by Publishers Group West

10 9 8 7 6 5 4 3

This book is dedicated to
all the Brown Baggers, Thursday Writers, and Marathoners
who have put pen to page
and to the spirit and memory of The Writing Center

"The writer, perhaps more than any of his fellow artists, has access to the human subconscious. His words sink deep, shaping dreams, easing the pain of loneliness, banishing incantations and omens, keeping alive the memories of the race, providing intimations of immortality, nourishing great anticipations, sharpening the instinct for justice, and imparting respect for the fragility of life. These functions are essential for human evolution. Without them, civilization becomes brittle and breaks easily. Society must be measured, therefore, not just by its display of power but by its attention to the conditions of creativity and its acceptance of human sovereignty as the highest value."

— Norman Cousins

# Contents

# Acknowledgments

If I wrote the names of all who had a part in this book, the acknowledgments section would outweigh the text. Because if I had my way, I would list every writer who participated in any of my writing-practice groups over the years, starting with my longtime friend Davenia Cray, who attended the very first session (and she's not even a writer). That not being possible, and though it doesn't feel sufficient, suffice to say that the hundreds of writers with whom I have written in the Tuesday and Thursday Brown Bag groups, the Thursday Writers' Group, all the Café Writers, and many, many Marathoners are part of the construction of this book and the spirit with which it is written.

My thanks go to:

Gina Misiroglu, my editor at New World Library whose vision expanded this book and who hand-held its transformation from whimsical to elegant.

Mary Ann Casler, for her inspired cover design.

Dale Fetherling, for his cheering on and his editing pencil, which he wields with a kind and generous hand.

John Fox, for reviewing the proposal and suggesting New World Library as a potential publisher. Chris Witt, for his early encouragement.

Arthur Campbell, both gracious and smart, who was on my side; Susan Shellcliffe, who made me look good; Pamela Underwood, whose art is here in spirit; and Deborah Parker, whose poetry is too.

The knowledgeable librarians at the central location of the San Diego Public Library and James Spring and Amy Wallen, who loaned me their books and more.

Members of the Question of the Week group, whose thoughtful opinions helped form the words on the cover.

Steve Montgomery, Ross Adams, and Cynthia Brooks, for love and celebration. Michelle Zive, for brave participation. Karen Swank, for staying the course and for her dreams. Greg Gorga and Mike Payton, because of time and friendship and words invested.

Leaving the specifics of this book, though it is impossible to separate one from the other, I am grateful to so many others who make my life rich beyond imagining.

Over the years I have had many writing teachers; the person who has finally given me the keys to the kingdom is Janet Fitch. Thanks and gratitude to my dear friend and best writing partner ever, Dian Greenwood, who continues to teach me so much about writing and life. Camille Stupar, who has traveled the road with me for so many years and who makes it a joyful and surprising ride. David Cohen, for his gifts of sight and insight. Alfred JaCoby, who has known me all along, for his unflagging friendship and enthusiasm. Drusilla Campbell, good friend, confidante, and colleague. Ray Bruce, who cofounded The Writing Center with me and whose encouragement and support long before and forever after have been as constant and solid as the mountains where he lives.

My children and their children where love has found a home — Chris and Stephanie, Alexandra and Andrew, Michael and Matthew, my daughter Amy, who fills my heart, and her partner, Paula. My sisters Janice, Sharon, and Jackie and their families, and my mother, who is finally able to read all she wants.

Finally, because it's the last paragraph and the one where a writer leaves what she hopes will be an enduring thought, I want to thank my friend and colleague of many years, Doris Doi, without whom this book could not have come to be.

# Introduction

"When I am writing I am doing
the thing I was meant to do."

—Anne Sexton

Last Tuesday at my regular Brown Bag Writing Group, the topic was "write about footprints." During the seventeen-minute exercise, Mimette described wild horses wheeling and galloping on the New Mexico range; Allison wrote about a woman who covered the entire expanse of her apartment's Berber carpeting with muddy prints as she arranged plants given her by her lovers; and Madeline began a story about a break-in and never did get to the part about the footprints. Greg's piece was about a tough kid from New Jersey who has appeared in more than a few of his practice pieces (he denies the character is based on any of his own East Coast exploits); Marcy sounded amazed at the juxtaposition of dead bodies and monkeys wearing shoes that turned up in her writing; Suzanna rhymed and twisted her way through a stream of consciousness piece that had us all laughing; and Juanita wrote a touching poem using footprints as a metaphor for prayers. I sketched out a partial scene for my novel with my characters leaving footprints in the dusty outdoor dance floor at a Lake of the Ozarks Saturday night fish fry. This time, Steve and Mike chose not to read their pieces.

We were together less than an hour, these nine writers and myself, a disparate group of musicians, bartenders, ex-marines, acupuncturists, landscapers, stay-at-home mothers, actresses, and retired nurses. After our session, we returned to our daily noontime routines, notebooks and spirits a little fuller for having written.

For more than five years, three and often four times a week, I have written in writing-practice groups. Sometimes we have been as few as two, other times we have numbered in the twenties. But the experience is always the same: We gather around a table or in easy chairs or on the floor or in the grass, a topic is given, and we fall into our notebooks. For the next five or ten or fifteen or twenty-two minutes the only sounds we hear are of pens gliding or scratching or spiraling across the page, sometimes a muffled sniffle or a suppressed giggle as the words work their way from birthing place to notebook cradle. The energy in the room is palpable; you can feel it sidling up against you, nuzzling your elbows. You can taste its electric hum. Sometimes, just for the quick thrill of it, I look up from my notebook at the bent heads, the moving hands. I love the sensation of being in the space of writers writing. These remarkable creators painting word pictures, spinning and reeling stories, remembering and recording, all aboard the magic ride of imagination. This is when I know I am in the right place, doing the thing I was meant to do. A giddy feeling comes upon me after we've all written and people begin to read — saying out loud this raw, wild, expansive creation of words on paper. I am amazed or entertained or transported from sadness to laughter to rollicking joy. We all are. I feel that pull of connection, not just one writer to another, but one human to another.

This experience of finding my tribe, of being home in the world isn't all I gain through these writing sessions, though it is more than enough and so much more than I anticipated or expected. One day I looked behind me and realized that over the years of regular writing practice, I had filled an astounding number of notebooks with my own original writing, page after blue-lined page of *my* writing. Not all of it good, mind you, but not all of it bad, either. In fact, some of it was surprisingly fresh, original, and full of energy. There were bits and pieces of stories, amusing characters named Sugar and Butch and Ruby Diamond, and a few others, some who were reminiscent of people I knew. Here were the bones of personal narrative essays and memories that amazed me in their careful detail. Some of the dialogue sounded as though some fifth-grader who just learned quotation marks composed it, but there were also a few startling exchanges that actually worked. Poems graced some of the pages. All this from a woman who, since third grade, wanted nothing more than to "be a writer," but who had, in actual truth, not written very much at all. Through these writing-practice sessions, alone and with others, I was finally producing on an ongoing, regular basis.

In rereading my tattered and shambled notebooks, I discovered images that reappeared month after month, stories that were told again and again, with different voices and in different settings, but the same recurring themes. The topic didn't seem to matter; my writing was telling me what I wanted (or needed) to write about. And this wasn't happening only to me; many of my writing-practice partners were having similar experiences.

Over the years that I have been leading and participating in writing-practice groups, and before that as a member of journal and women's writing groups, I've come to accept the phenomenon that happens when people join together to write. Call it a collective energy, the creative force. Magic. I say the Muse likes to work crowds. And so, because of my own extraordinary experience, I urge writers to write together, in twos and fours and more. Whatever the room will hold. I take writers all over the countryside and stage all kinds of workshops so we can write in community.

But I also know that given a topic to write on, a notebook to write in, and time devoted to doing the work, anyone can be a writer who writes.

In 1993, I cofounded, with Ray Bruce, The Writing Center in San Diego. TWC was a nonprofit literary arts organization whose purpose was to encourage and nurture the development of creative writers, and to promote a literary community. Unfortunately, like many nonprofit arts organizations, funding was difficult to find and, after just five years of operation, we were forced to close, leaving an enormous void in the community. It was during those hectic and romantic five years that I came to know this: many who want to be writers — who are in their hearts, writers — have followed the same beaten path that doesn't come to a dead end so much as it peters out.

At the beginning of every class, I ask my students to talk about their experience with writing and themselves as writers. Shannon's story is the same as Josie's, as Don's, as Lori's, as Gilbert's, as Lila's, as a hundred others I can name. It goes like this.

> "I always wanted to be a writer. I started writing when I was really young. Poems and stories, little pieces. But I could never finish anything. I'd put it all away and wouldn't write for a while. But then, something would make me want to start again. So I'd write more stories and poems. I even started a novel once. But I'd get busy doing something else and drift away from it. Now here I am 37 years old. I hate my job and feel like something is missing from my life. And I want to write again."

These students and others, whose stories differ in only some of the details, have one thing in common: even though their spirit longs for it, they have never made writing a priority in their lives; that is, they have never set aside a special, specific time for their writing. They don't practice their craft.

    This book came about because I saw the difference ongoing, regular practice could make in a writer's life. I saw it not only in the lives of my students, but I experienced it in my own life. This is what I know: By integrating regular writing-practice sessions into your life, notebooks will get filled, stories will be written, or poems or whatever surprising forms your writing takes. Your writing will improve and so will the quality of your life. That irresistible urge that brought you to the page in the first place will be fulfilled. The longing stilled. Even if you continue to need a day job to support yourself — and most of us will — your spirit will be glad.

    I also found that it's easier to begin the writing when a prompt is supplied — like someone providing the music when you want to dance. So this book contains a writing-practice topic for every day of the year plus a few extras. Many of these topics have been used by the Tuesday Brown Baggers or the Thursday Writers' Group, or in any of a dozen writing marathons. I've written to most of them myself. They are all guaranteed to work if you give yourself over to them, trust the process, and follow your pen.

    During the months of writing this book, a recurring fantasy appeared. It was this: At a certain hour on a certain day, everyone who was using this book would look up the topic for that day. And for the next eighteen minutes, all of us — just-beginning writers, longtime dyed-in-the-wool writers, wordsmiths, amateurs, professionals, cynics, and true believers — all of us would sit down, open our notebooks, and write together.

                                 Judy Reeves,
                                 San Diego, CA
                                 March 12, 1999

# How to Use This Book

"To write is to write is to write is to write is to write is to write is to write."

—Gertrude Stein

A stranger to New York City, looking for directions, asks a man on the street, "How do I get to Carnegie Hall?"

"Practice, man," comes the response.

It's an old joke, but the truth is there. In order to get good at anything, you've got to practice. So when somebody asks me, How do I write a novel? Or a short story? An essay, poem, or book? I give them the same answer as that man on the street: *Practice. Practice. Practice.*

This idea of writing practice is a new concept to many who want to write. Sure, everybody knows pianists have to train. So do dancers, actors, singers, and athletes. Even artists have sketchbooks, which serve as their practice pages. But there seems to be some vague notion that somewhere deep inside the desire to be a writer is the inherent knowledge of how to go about it. As many a bloody-fingered would-be writer, hip-deep in wadded up paper and frustration can attest, this just ain't so.

Natural talent and all the breaks in the world notwithstanding, to become good at anything you've got to do the drills. Lots of drills. To quote Mick Jagger, "You have to sing every day so you can build up to being, you know, Amazingly Brilliant."

## What Is Writing Practice

Writing practice is showing up at the page. It's running the scales, executing the movements. It's writing for the experience of it, forming the words, capturing the images, filling the pages. Like an artist's sketchbook, a writer's notebook is filled with perspectives, character sketches, shadings, and tones. A writing workout is trying out phrases and auditioning words, letting the imagination have free rein while the editor in your head takes a coffee break. One of the best things about writing practice is that it *is* practice. It's not supposed to be perfect. You're free to make mistakes, fool around, take risks.

When you show up at the page and put in the time day after day, you learn to trust your pen and the voice that emerges as your own. You name yourself Writer.

This is what happens: By taking the time for writing practice, you are honoring yourself as writer. When you write on a daily basis, your self-confidence increases. You learn what you want to write about and what matters to you as a writer. You explore your creative nooks and crannies, and make forays into some scary places that make your hand tremble and your heart beat faster. This is good. This is when you know you are writing your truth, and that's the best writing anybody ever does. In writing practice, you poke around in your psyche; you grieve and heal and discover things about yourself you never knew. And this is the truth: your writing really does get better.

## Make a Commitment by Making the Time

Talking about writing isn't the same as writing. Anyone who has promised herself she'd go to the gym today "no matter what" then finds herself still in her office clothes at 10 P.M. knows this. "I'll do it tomorrow," the would-be exerciser says day after day, just like the would-be writer.

*Eighty percent of success is showing up.*
— Woody Allen

The way to make a commitment to writing practice is to make an appointment with your writer-self and keep it — same as you would an appointment with your dentist or your best friend. Write in your daily calendar the time each day you plan to write. Ten minutes or two hours. Write it down. Then do it.

Getting into a regular practice groove may take a few test runs. You may schedule mornings when nights are really better. If you commit to two hours every day, but find yourself stressed-out and hating the idea of writing practice and going to the page with a Godzilla-sized grudge, or, worse yet, not going at all, reconsider how much time you can really commit. Be flexible. Create a schedule that works for you, so that when practice time comes, you accept it as an ongoing, necessary part of your life as a writer and look forward to it as a gift to yourself.

You may have to change your appointment. Certainly there will be days when, no matter what, you simply have to cancel. When this happens, do it consciously and with intention. Just as you would call your dentist or best friend to reschedule rather than standing them up, tell yourself why you have to postpone or change the appointment, and set a time for another meeting. Your writer-self deserves this consideration.

## Writing-Practice Topics

Many writing practitioners, when they sit down to write, freeze. "I don't know what to write about," they say, while holding the pen in a death grip somewhere down near the nib. Truth is, each of us has so much we want to write about, a deluge of ideas, memories, and images, that we can become paralyzed by infinite choice. The brain simply can't make up its mind so it launches into what it does best: measuring, judging, calculating. Thinking. The worst possible thing for writing practice.

This is why I've included suggested writing topics for each day of the year. The topics are located on the right-hand page throughout the book. To use this book, simply locate the date, write the topic for that day at the top of a blank page in your notebook, grab the first image that comes to you, and write it. No matter what the topic, what you want to write about will emerge on the page. Story seedlings, poetic uprisings, character visitations — things that are deep inside are brought to the surface by the focus and energy and freewheeling fearlessness of writing practice.

When you write from the topics, feel free to change the tense — past to present or vice versa — or the point of view. If the topic uses "you," this doesn't mean you have to write about yourself. Change the pronoun to "he" or "she," or use a character's name (or a real person, if you want). Use the prompts to write from a character's point of view; create a fragment or work on a scene for a longer piece. Write fiction, memoir, essay. Mix the genres; find your writer's groove, then ride it.

The writing topics are expressed in several ways — as sentence stems, quotes, directives, or simply phrases or words.

For example, the topic for January 16 is a simple, straightforward directive: *Write about a bed.* If the first image that comes to you is the bed you slept in when you were 16 in your messy, book-strewn teenage bedroom with the jonquil wallpaper, write about that bed. Begin anywhere — going to sleep, waking up, changing the sheets, hiding beneath the covers. If you're writing a fictional piece, write about a bed from a character's point of view, whatever bed the character "sees." Write an essay on beds, a homage to beds, an ode to your lover's bed, or a list poem of beds you have slept in (or not). The invitation is as broad as a king-size mattress and as unlimited as anything you might dream thereon.

The topic for March 28 is a sentence stem: *"The last time I saw _____."* Because the prompt is set in quotes, it invites you to use the sentence as

*I am entitled to tell this particular story in a way no one else can.*

— Amy Hempel

dialogue, but you don't have to write dialogue. Simply begin with the sentence stem, fill in the blank with the first image that comes to you, and be off on a ten-minute romp through a city, with a person, on a riverboat, at the theater, or in the company of your favorite nephew or the ice cream vendor.

On November 14, a line from a poem by Wislawa Szymborska is used: *"The window had other views."* Throughout the book, great writers are quoted, sometimes, as in this case, with a line for a writing prompt. When writing from this topic, it's not necessary to actually use the line in your writing. Use instead the images it suggests, looking out the windows of your memory or imagination, or the window you sit before as you write. Of course, you can use the line anywhere in the piece, even as a line of dialogue or the lead-in to start your writing.

*It's all about letting the story take over.*

— Robert Stone

*You're in the backseat of a taxi* is the prompt for March 19. This topic can be written from the second person (you), or it can be about yourself (a memory of being in the backseat of a taxi), or it can be about a fictional character. Again, take the image that comes from the prompt, without taking the prompt too literally.

One more example: the topic for January 13 is *After midnight*. The lack of any directive (*write about, describe, remember*) is intentional. You're free to use the actual words as the beginning of a sentence, or to find inspiration in the idea of "after midnight," as a time, space, feeling, or image. Or write an after midnight memory.

Prompts aren't themes for compositions or essays. They're not topics you must stay with, as in "stick to the topic." The idea is not to think about what the prompts mean or how to interpret them. Just start writing. The freedom to let your writing go down any open road is one of the delights of writing to suggested topics. You don't even have to use the prompt itself!

Different writers respond to different invitations. Some writers resonate with concrete images, others like abstract. And often, the less said about a prompt, the more wide-open the invitation for the intuitive to work. A sentence stem one day, an evocative quote the next, sometimes just an image — this variety stimulates writerly interest and keeps the prompts fresh. Don't worry about "doing it right." The good news is there's no way to do it wrong. Simply read the prompt, trust the image, and begin writing.

You can use the topics again and again; different images will emerge, memories will rise, fresh ideas will form, and you'll keep writing. After some time, you'll be able to reread your notebooks and notice themes and recurring images. This is another gift of writing practice: You'll discover what matters to you as a writer, what you are passionate about.

An important note about the topics: Don't reject the topic out of hand or consider what you're going to write about before you begin. Find the topic, note it at the top of your page, and begin writing. If you stop to think, you'll run the risk of talking yourself out of what might be a rich vein for writing-practice mining.

## The Book of Days

The book is divided into months, with each of the twelve months containing a profusion of writerly counsel and advice, words of inspiration, and literary lore and legend. Each month begins with one of twelve "Guidelines for Writing Practice" that are just that: guidelines to help you along the writing-practice road. Some of these may sound familiar. Concepts like "keep writing" and "don't worry about the rules" are presented in any number of books on the craft. They're not original, but they are basic to creating a solid foundation on which to build your daily work.

You'll also find hundreds of rousing exercises on everything from auditioning words to using your dreams in your writing. You'll find out how to build your own writing community and how to say yes to the Muse. Tips and how-tos help you discover places to practice, reveal what matters to you as a writer, and show you how to translate real life into fiction. Easy-to-use checklists expose the telltale signs that let you know when the critic, the censor, or the editor are having their way with your writing. Subjects are cross-referenced so you can easily find related information.

Throughout the book, the experience, wisdom, opinions, and even a few quirks and idiosyncrasies of a number of well-known writers are presented in "The Writing Life." This monthly feature brings to the fore such unlikely information as how these writers courted the Muse to what they dreamed about and how they supported themselves on their way to becoming full-time writers.

*I put a piece of paper under my pillow, and when I could not sleep I wrote in the dark.*

— Henry David
    Thoreau

## Beyond Practice

Closing out each month is "Beyond Practice" — special invitations for writers to treat themselves. Consider these a reward, a bonus, if you will. Dividends for hard work and hanging in. With titles such as Café Writing; On the Road; Hot Nights/Wild Women; and A Jug of Wine, a Loaf of Bread — a Notebook, these twelve self-directed miniworkshops encourage writing practitioners to set aside a once-a-month special session to honor themselves as writer and nourish the writing-self. Alone or with the friendly company of other writers, the sessions take participants outside the margins of daily practice and into the wider world that exists beyond practice. They are to have fun, to play, to expand possibilities, and explore the further reaches. Evocative in and of themselves, each session features a handful of bonus writing topics. Enjoy.

*It is my heart that makes songs, not I.*
— Sara Teasdale

## The Effects of Writing Practice

I've been leading writing-practice groups for over five years, two and three times a week, and writing marathons that run long hours, and I always write along with the others. I have also participated in countless practice sessions alone, with various writing partners, and with a mélange of writing groups. Here's what I know:

On any given day, a writer can write the best she's ever written, or she can compose a piece that's clunky and misshapen and downright embarrassing in its black-and-white awfulness. Practice isn't about being a good writer or a bad writer, it's about being present with the writing, surrendering to the process, and trusting the pen.

At any given practice session, we are all beginners.

Through writing practice, I have been invited to participate in a community where I am free to be all that I am as writer — insecure, self-conscious, ungraceful, passionate, raw, reckless, wild, and even outside my self. I have found my own kind.

By showing up at the page and doing the writing, I, and other writers, have filled hundreds of notebooks. We have started and completed short stories, plays, novels, essays, memoirs, gifts of writing for others, and, wondrously, we have even experienced the appearance of poems. We've claimed ourselves as writers.

If you will practice every day, and be gentle with yourself, you may be amazed. Your writing will be fresher, livelier, more spontaneous. You will take more risks, write more passionately, and reach into places you didn't know existed. Ideas and images and language with brilliant plumage will parade on the page before your eyes. Then one day, after a particularly surprising session, you will read what you have written, shake your head in astonishment, and say, "Where did that come from?" And you will know, it came from *you*.

## Guidelines for Writing Practice

1. Keep writing. Don't stop to edit, to rephrase, to think. Don't go back and read what you've written until you've finished.

2. Trust your pen. Go with the first image that appears.

3. Don't judge your writing. Don't compare, analyze, criticize.

4. Let your writing find its own form. Allow it to organically take shape into a story, an essay, a poem, dialogue, an incomplete meander.

5. Don't worry about the rules. Don't worry about grammar, syntax, punctuation, or sentence structure.

6. Let go of expectations. Let your writing surprise you.

7. *Kiss your frogs.* Remember, this is just practice. Not every session will be magic. The point is to just suit up and show up at the page, no matter what.

8. Tell the truth. Be willing to go to the scary places that make your hand tremble and your handwriting get a little out of control. Be willing to tell your secrets.

9. Write accurate details. Your writing doesn't have to be factual, but the specificity of the details brings it alive. The truth isn't in the facts; it's in the detail.

10. Write what matters. If you don't care about what you're writing, neither will your readers. Be a passionate writer.

11. Read your writing aloud after you've completed your practice session. You'll find out what you've written, what you care about, when you're writing the truth, and when the writing is "working."

12. Date your page and write the topic at the top. This will keep you grounded in the present and help you reference pieces you might want to use in something else. ❧

# JANUARY

"I heard an angel
    speak last night,
        And he said, 'write!'"

—Elizabeth Barrett Browning

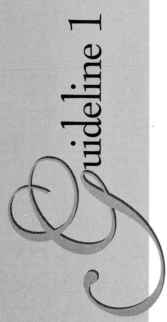

## Keep Writing

The most important part of writing practice is writing. Getting the words down on the page. Don't stop to edit, to think, to rephrase, or rewrite. If you keep your writing hand moving, you'll bypass the censor, the editor, the critic, and if you're lucky, maybe even the ego.

This isn't to say writing practice is "stream-of-consciousness" writing where you attempt to get down every thought that passes through your mind and the writing that emerges is a jumble of disconnected thoughts and images. During practice sessions, stay focused on the topic and the image that arises, and keep the pen moving as it explores that image and then moves on to the next. Sometimes you'll rocket through the topic on a surge of power that started at liftoff and keeps you at 4Gs the whole ride; other times your writing will be more like a lazy river on a Sunday afternoon, peaceful and easy and sundappled. The trick is to, at any speed, just keep writing till the end.

Don't stop to reread what you've written until you've completed the practice session. Each time you stop, you move out of the place of intuitive trusting to a cerebral place of judging, evaluating, comparing. There is a time for that, but not during practice sessions. Writing practice is for writing.

Just keep the pen moving until the time is up, or until you feel complete.

## How to Start

You've set aside the time, you're sitting in the place you've chosen to do today's practice session, and you're comfortable. Maybe you're with a writing friend. Pen and notebook are at hand and you're ready to begin writing. Here's what you do:

Date your page, find the topic for today's session, and write it at the top of your page. Then, before you start to think about how you want to approach the topic, simply grab the tail of the first image that sailed into your mind when you wrote it down, and begin writing. Let the words spill from your pen easily and naturally. Don't worry about staying in the lines; don't worry about spelling, punctuation, or grammar. Don't worry about anything. Just write. When you come to a natural slowdown, ease your grip on your pen (you may be surprised at how tightly you're holding on). Breathe. Let the next image come to you. It may be an extension of the first image or it may be something new that was born out of what you've been writing. Whatever image appears, don't resist, just fall into it, and keep writing.

Above all else, don't stop to think and don't go back and reread what you've written. If you can't think of the name of a place or a person or some other fact, make up something or draw a line. If you run into a blank wall, rewrite the topic, repeat the last line you wrote, or write "I don't know what to write next." If you keep the pen moving, you'll find your place again. Just keep writing until the time is up or until you feel complete. If you can, read your piece aloud after you've finished. *(See Guideline 11.)*

Congratulate yourself. You honored your commitment to practice and, by doing so, you honored yourself as writer. If it didn't go as smoothly as you wanted, don't worry. There's always tomorrow. And tomorrow and tomorrow.

*Every morning or afternoon, whenever you want to write, you have to go up and shoot that old bear under your desk between the eyes.*

—Robert Leckie

### Writing Topics

| | |
|---|---|
| January 1 | Write about Sunday afternoon. |
| January 2 | Write about a time someone said no. |
| January 3 | You're standing in a doorway. |
| January 4 | "A year after your death, … " (after Czeslaw Milosz) |

*You've got to get into the process. The process is liberating. The process is good. You take it word by word. You take it day by day. And you have to not worry too much.*

—Robert Stone

## Tools for Writing Practice

Tools for the writer are simple: pen and paper. Inexpensive, portable, and replenishable. Some writers can be downright obsessive about their tools — only a certain paper, a particular pen, anything else and they're off their game.

Consider this: In a writing-practice session of fifteen minutes you might write 450 words, more or less, or three to four pages. You'll do this every day. Up to as many as 100 pages a month. (The size of your writing, the size of the notebook, the length of the practice session — all these are factors.) Because of the sheer quantity of paper, most practice writers use inexpensive, spiral-bound notebooks. Wide ruled. But the choice is yours. Find a notebook you're comfortable with, one that fits your writing style and your budget.

Regarding pens or pencils. Remember, you'll be writing along at a fairly good speed; you'll want a pen that doesn't skip or resist the paper, or bleed through to the other side. Always have a spare. Nothing is more frustrating than to run out of ink in the midst of it all.

Writing practice is best done by hand.

## Why Write by Hand

Ah, what technology has brought us! First the typewriter, then the word processor, now the computer, even the voice-recognition computer. Why write by hand when there's all this technology, the nanosecond response to the very flick of the finger, the ability to alter sentences, relocate paragraphs, erase, or rearrange whole chapters with macro magic. And how our fingers fly. At last we can almost keep up with our thoughts. With all this, why still write by hand?

Legions of writers still do, and for their own good reasons. For example: feminist scholar and writer bell hooks said there's something about handwriting that slows the idea process. When working on the computer, she said, "you don't have those moments of pause that you need." Writer and monologist Spalding Gray believes writing by hand is the closest thing he can get to his breath, and novelist Anne Tyler said the muscular movement of putting down script on the paper gets her imagination back in the track where it was. Master horror writer Clive Barker said that for him, handwriting is "the most direct association I can make between what's going on in my mind's eye and what's going to appear on the page."

The following are more reasons to write by hand.

*The typewriter separated me from a deeper intimacy with poetry, and my hand brought me closer to that intimacy again.*
— Pablo Neruda

- Writing is a physical act; you should do it with your body.
- Writing muscles include the hand and the heart.
- Writing by hand is sensual; it allows you to feel the movement of pen against paper.
- You can feel your heart beat when you write by hand; sometimes you can feel your pulse in your fingers.

| | |
|---|---|
| January 5 | Write about a day moon. |
| January 6 | Write about bathing. |
| January 7 | Once, when no one was looking … |
| January 8 | It's what I do in the middle of the night. |
| January 9 | Write about a ceremony. |

■ Writing by hand allows you to write with your breath.

■ When you write by hand you slow down enough to write only *some* of your thoughts. In writing practice more is not necessarily better.

■ You are more connected to your feelings when you write by hand.

■ Handwriting is alive.

■ You are in control when you write by hand (no low battery or malfunction or save command or crash can interrupt you).

■ You can write anywhere when you write by hand.

Writing by hand is elemental to writing practice. Even if you feel most at home at your computer, fingers flinging words onto the screen, I urge you to slow down, pick up what the versatile and prolific writer John Updike called "the humblest and quietest of weapons, a pencil" and try a month's worth of practice-writing by hand. ❧

*I've always had a very comfortable relationship with No. 2 pencils.*

—William Styron

## Desks and Spaces

**Rita Dove** said she loves the absolute quiet of her cabin in the woods. It's "the silence of the world," she said, "birds shifting weight on branches, the branches squeaking against other twigs, the deer *hooosching* through the woods...."

**Amy Tan** surrounds herself with objects that carry with them a personal history — old books, bowls and boxes, chairs and benches from imperial China.

**Richard Ford's** desk is more of a concept than a thing. "It's like the 'Belize desk' at the State Department; an idea more than a place you actually sit at."

**Annie Dillard** recommended a room with no view, "so imagination can meet memory in the dark."

**Kurt Vonnegut** uses his hardwood floor as a "desk" where he spreads and piles and keeps things near at hand as he works from his lap while seated on a padded Danish walnut easy chair.

**Susan Sontag** spreads her writing and reference materials across a long table with benches along either side.

The bed served as desk for any number of writers including **Walker Percy, Edith Wharton, Colette, Marcel Proust,** and **James Joyce.**

"Our task," wrote **John Updike,** "is to rise above the setting, with its comforts and distractions, into a relationship with our ideal reader...."

The *Writing Life*

| | |
|---|---|
| January 10 | Write about a wound. |
| January 11 | You are in a motel room. |
| January 12 | Write about acceptable losses. |
| January 13 | After midnight. |
| January 14 | Write about the horizon. |

## "Belief & Technique for Modern Prose — List of Essentials"

### By Jack Kerouac

1. Scribbled secret notebooks, and wild typewritten pages, for yr own joy
2. Submissive to everything, open, listening
3. Try never get drunk outside yr own house
4. Be in love with yr life
5. Something that you feel will find its own form
6. Be crazy dumbsaint of the mind
7. Blow as deep as you want to blow
8. Write what you want bottomless from bottom of the mind
9. The unspeakable vision of the individual
10. No time for poetry but exactly what is
11. Visionary tics shivering in the chest
12. In tranced fixation dreaming upon object before you
13. Remove literary, grammatical and syntactical inhibition
14. Like Proust, be an old teahead of time
15. Telling the true story of the world in interior monolog
16. The jewel center of interest is the eye within the eye
17. Write in recollection and amazement for yourself
18. Work from pithy middle eye out, swimming in language sea
19. Accept loss forever
20. Believe in the holy contour of life
21. Struggle to sketch the flow that already exists intact in mind
22. Dont [sic] think of words when you stop but to see picture better
23. Keep track of every day the date emblazoned in yr morning
24. No fear or shame in the dignity of yr experience, language & knowledge
25. Write for the world to read and see yr exact pictures of it
26. Bookmovie is the movie in words, the visual American form
27. In Praise of Character in the Bleak inhuman Loneliness
28. Composing wild, undisciplined, pure, coming in from under, crazier the better
29. You're a Genius all the time
30. Writer-Director of Earthly movies Sponsored & Angeled in Heaven

As ever, Jack

## How to Create a Space of Your Own

Every writer needs a place to call her or his own, whether it's a folding table behind a screen in the bedroom or a separate studio with desk, computer, napping couch, and window with a view. Find yours and claim it. Furnish it with those things that give you comfort, inspire you, support you. Make it a safe space, a place you go to joyfully. Writing is creating and creating is work/play for the soul.

Your writing space doesn't have to be a fixed location, nor does it have to be the only place you write. Throughout this book are suggestions to make your writing mobile. More than a few writers need the stimulation of public places to get their writing done, especially first-draft writing. At a workshop, author Naomi Epel talked about schlepping her grocery cart loaded with laptop computer, manuscript, references books, and pages of notes to cafés all over Berkeley. And one gray-haired writer has become an afternoon fixture at the window table of The Living Room Café in San Diego where he opens his briefcase, spreads out his papers, and sets up his writing desk. Even individuals who come to weekly writing-practice groups have claimed squatter's rights to their own space at the table and always sit in the same chair with the same accoutrements of water bottle or caffé latte or rainbow of pens arrayed before them.

What you need in a writing space is safety and comfort, both psychic and physical; a place where you feel free to lose yourself in the world you are creating on paper.

*See Places to Practice, Practice Accoutrements*

*The requirement of any writing space is that it disappear from the mind's eye of the inhabitant.*

—John Updike

| | |
|---|---|
| January 15 | It's Saturday afternoon. You're not at home. |
| January 16 | Write about a bed. |
| January 17 | Write about a time you found out about something you weren't supposed to know. |
| January 18 | "It was noon and nothing is concluded." (after Donald Rawley) |

## Writer's Notebooks

Every writer needs one. This is the place you put all that stuff that comes to you while you're focused on something else. It's the workbench for cobbling together bits and pieces or to fix part of your story that is not working.

A writer's notebook is the receptacle for ideas and trying out words and images. A place for making notes to yourself.

Some writers keep separate notebooks for recordings of the senses, descriptions of the weather, character sketches, bits of dialogue, and other subjects. They write everything down in their current, working notebook, then from time to time, transfer pieces into the separate notebooks. These they file on a shelf near their desk. When they need a description of an August sky in Aspen, they finger through their Landscapes notebook till *voila!* just the entry that works: Aspen, August 14, 1997 — and there follows the color of sky, the shape of the clouds with metaphor abounding, the sound of shadow on mountain, light-footed and nimble.

A writer's notebook is what you always carry with you. Along with your pen. Howard Junker, editor of the literary journal *Zyzzyva*, describes his pocket-sized version as his "stealth" notebook and suggests you have one, too. Best-selling author and writing guru Anne Lamott stuffs three-by-five-inch cards in her back pocket for scribbling down that which comes to her as she walks the dog or is otherwise away from her desk. She also writes on her body, messy but apparently effective.

Writer's notebooks lean toward the chaotic. Unless they're airlifted out, jottings tend to get recorded and forgotten, like last year's Christmas cards. Robin Hemley, author and editor of the journal *Bellingham Review*, suggests leafing back through your notebook (he calls his a journal) from time to time. Like panning for gold, you might get nuggets and you might get gravel. But then again, you could be making a driveway and a few loads of gravel is just what you need.

*You can't sit around thinking. You have to sit around writing.*

—David Long

## Daily Routine

Imagine that you put off brushing your teeth until you could spend some really serious time doing it, or that every day you waited to drive to work until you felt inspired to do so. Okay, so these are ridiculous comparisons, but the point is when something is part of your daily routine, you don't struggle with doing it, you simply build it into your schedule and do it. The suggestion here is to make writing a part of your routine — just like brushing your teeth and driving to work.

1. Making writing a part of your daily routine means it will be easier to write. Postponing until you can get in some "really good hours" often translates into not writing at all — something always seems to come up. Or, the stress of "have to" writing blocks any really good work.

A daily writing routine means that when those long stretches of writing time — weekends, holidays, vacations — come, you can slip as easily into the time as a floppy disk into an A drive. Plus, you have all that raw material to work with.

2. When you make an appointment for a writing time, you don't have to struggle with the "should" or "ought" of writing, or make the decision to write or not write; you just do it. You honor the appointment with your writer-self as much as you would an appointment with your doctor, your business partner, or your best friend.

3. Just because Ernest Hemingway believed he had to get to work before the sun rose doesn't mean you have to. Set your daily routine for writing at the

*What is important? Living as active a life as possible, meeting all ranks of people, plenty of travel, trying your hand at various kinds of work, keeping your eyes, ears, and mind open, remembering what you observe, reading plenty of good books, and writing every day — simply writing.*

— Edward Abbey

| | |
|---|---|
| January 19 | Remember a sound. |
| January 20 | Look out your window; write what you see. |
| January 21 | Write about something you bought mail order. |
| January 22 | In the meantime … |
| January 23 | Write a love letter. To anyone. |

• • • • • • • • • • • • • • • • • • • • • • • • • • • • • • • • • • • • • • • • • •

time that suits you best, not when everyone else says you should.

If you're an early riser, do your writing practice in the morning, when you first awaken. Stay in bed and write under the covers if you want. But if you need a few cups of coffee before you can even hold a pen, by all means have them. Some of us even like to start projects at ten o'clock at night and work into the wee hours.

Find a time when the work flows easily and naturally, when you write instead of edit. Make this your practice time.

4. For a change, vary your daily writing time to catch yourself in different moods, with different energy. Especially if you feel yourself or your writing getting into a rut.

*I'm one of those people that believes you should start writing before you think you're ready.*

—Joseph Ellis

Guaranteed: A daily routine that includes writing will have more benefits than you can imagine, but just for starters (a) the writing will come easier, (b) you'll write more, (c) your writing will improve, and (d) you'll realize that you are, after all, a writer. ❧

*See The Discipline of Writing*

## How Can You Tell When Imagination Is Present?

Someone said all you need to be a writer is an imagination and curiosity. (Add to that stamina.) Your imagination is in the unique, individual way you see the world, the particular and specific details you notice, and the connections you make. More than merely your experience, it is the way you contemplate and interpret your experience. The great novelist Henry James said, "It [experience] is the very atmosphere of the mind; and when the mind is imaginative … it takes to itself the faintest hints of life, it converts the very pulses of air into revelations."

How can you tell if the imagination is present, not only in your writing but also in your life?

*You can't depend on your eyes when your imagination is out of focus.*

— Mark Twain

■ You feel a strong urge to create — to write, to paint, to play music, to dance, to make art.

■ Your writing is bold, full of passion and life. "Violent passions emit the Real, Good and Perfect tones," poet William Blake said.

■ You experience great freedom in your writing, leaping from image to image as if your words were Baryshnikov and your notebook the stage.

■ You work innocently, not from the ego and not to please or impress.

■ You are comfortable doing nothing. For long stretches of time.

■ You trust your writing and your experience.

■ You live in the present moment because you know that is where imagination will look for you.

■ You meander rather than stride calisthenically; you notice the form and colors of leaves, the shape of clouds, the curve of hill.

| | |
|---|---|
| January 24 | Write about leaving. |
| January 25 | Shadows. |
| January 26 | Describe the contents of someone's closet. |
| January 27 | Write about a used car. |

- Your writing (and your life) surprises you.
- You try some new thing rather than doing the same old tried and true — even if it was great.
- You believe you will never run out of ideas.
- You don't plan what you are going to do, you just do it; the planning comes later.
- You go forth (in your writing and your life) with no fear.
- You gaze out windows for long periods of time and stare into treetops; you've been accused of daydreaming.
- You write new, raw, wild stuff instead of rewriting the same piece endlessly.
- You converse about your characters as if they were fully alive.
- You are completely yourself. That's when ideas come, according to the great composer Wolfgang Amadeus Mozart, who knew these things.
- You make up things with the abandon of a child. Spontaneity thrills you.
- You write without the need to prove anything.
- You live your life fully, submerge yourself completely in the experience of it.
- You cannot force imagination to be present, but if you are in no hurry, "free, good-natured and at ease," it will appear, according to writer Brenda Ueland, who said, "The imagination is always searching in us and trying to free what we really think." ❧

 *See Imagination and Other Surprises*

*Writing is a kind of free fall that you then go back and edit and shape.*

—Allan Gurganus

## A Writing Date

Writing with someone else changes the energy of practice sessions. Another person can offer moral support, a friendly ear for your words, and companionship for those times when writing solo is just too lonely. Writing with someone else and reading your work aloud to each other creates a kind of intimacy, a writerly friendship that's unlike any other.

Invite a writing friend or someone you know from a writing workshop for a writing date. Cafés are good meeting places, as are parks or other outdoor settings. The absence of homelife distractions and the benefit of being in neutral territory make public spaces better than individual homes for this sort of date. If you choose a restaurant, make sure the proprietor looks kindly on the lengthy occupation of his table that a writing date implies. Allow a couple of hours.

Naturally you'll want to chat first, catch up on any news, and get comfortable in the space and with each other. But set a limit for your chatting. All talking and no writing do not a writing date make.

Each of you can bring prewritten writing prompts (three each), or jot them down as you prepare to write. Commingle the topics in the center of the table (written on a small strip of paper, folded to conceal the contents); select one and write for five minutes. After each person has read aloud what they've written, select another topic and write for ten minutes, then do a fifteen-minute, a ten-minute, and a five-minute session, reading after each writing.

Begin a completely new piece with each prompt or continue the same piece using each new prompt to alter the course of your writing.

Over the course of the forty-five minutes that you write together, you may

| | |
|---|---|
| January 28 | Write about "the sky you were born under." (after Joy Harjo) |
| January 29 | The end of the day. |
| January 30 | Write about a forbidden activity. |
| January 31 | "The first time I wore _____." |

notice that your writing has informed one another's. You may pick up images from one another's writing, and it's not unusual for each person to write an identical or similar image or use the same unique word like *pomegranate* or *grandiose.* Call it coincidence if you want.

A writing date doesn't have to be limited to two people. Invite three or four for a session. More than five and it becomes a party rather than a date.

Here are some topics you can use:

- Things you know without asking.
- Write about getting up in the morning.
- Write about stolen moments.
- "I told you stories about …"
- Sometimes she forgets what she wants.

# FEBRUARY

"You must travel at random, like the first Mayans. You must risk getting lost in the thickets, but that is the only way to make art."

—Tezcatillipoca

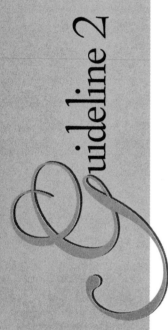

## Trust Your Pen

At the first reading of a writing-practice topic, an image will appear. You can trust this image. Poet Allen Ginsberg was quoting the great Buddhist master Chögyam Trungpa Rinpoche when he reminded us, "first thought, best thought." This first thought comes from your intuitive mind, where the creative process finds its foothold and the ego holds no sway. This is the place of rich images and deep thoughts.

Grasp your pen lightly and let come what wants to come. Follow your pen as it writes the image, word by single word. You may sense some rush to get on to the next image, but there's no hurry. Take a breath and let your pen roam freely within the boundaries of the first image while you ride along. Then write the next image and the next. Out of this, an order will organically arise, one that you would have missed had you rushed headlong from one image to the next.

Again Ginsberg: "It is necessary to resort to some very crude and rapid method of notation to sketch some fleeting sensory detail of this process of myriad sensations running thru the Being.... I do not know what I do. I get lost. I tell lies. I follow what comes in my mind next."

The pen is the tool of the intuitive. It won't take you further or deeper than you want to go, but it might take you to uncharted places you never thought about consciously.

## Timed Writings

When I first began doing writing-practice sessions with other writers, we set a time for our writing, probably to give structure to the session more than anything else. However, over the years, I discovered that setting a time limit has many other, more beneficial effects than simply creating structure.

1. It becomes easier to actually do the writing ("anybody can write for ten or fifteen minutes").

2. A tension is created that enables you to focus.

3. The writer is allowed to forget himself and be present with the writing.

4. It evokes spontaneity; there's no time to think or ponder.

5. It keeps the writing moving forward to the next word instead of rewriting, reconsidering, rethinking.

6. With an end in sight, it's easier to begin.

7. There's freedom in knowing you don't have to finish, you just stop when the time is up. Consequently, you can take more risks.

8. Writing time can easily be fit into a too full schedule.

9. Writing that doesn't work or isn't interesting can be abandoned when the time's up.

10. On the other hand, that same writing can turn interesting if pursued for the full amount of time allotted.

It's not necessary to use timed writings for every practice session, especially when you're writing alone. You may find yourself writing for an hour or more without looking up from the page, and who knows what you might lose if you stop just because of an arbitrary time limit. I say, when you're hot you're hot and if you're cooking keep writing, no matter what.

*Those rituals of getting ready to write produce a kind of trance.*

— John Barth

### Writing Topics

| | |
|---|---|
| February 1 | Write about a kiss. |
| February 2 | Find your way in a city. |
| February 3 | These are the things women know about love. |
| February 4 | Write about a black-and-white photograph. |

*Learn to listen when
you're talking to people.
Listen to how people say
things, to what they really
mean, because people
frequently say one thing
and mean another. Learn
to separate the wheat
from the chaff and look
at your own poetry the
same way.*

— Nikki Giovanni

## Pay Attention

Do you remember what you had for breakfast this morning? Can you describe the texture of moonlight on your bedroom ceiling or the face of the old man down the street as he walked his dog? "The truth is in the details," someone once said, and the only way to know the truth is to pay attention.

Paying attention brings into focus the specificity not only of good writing, but also of mindful living. The great spiritual leader Thich Nhat Hanh said mindfulness is to be present in the present moment. It is in the present moment you find the details that will enrich your writing and bring it to life. "There is ecstasy in paying attention," said Anne Lamott.

As you awaken in the morning, notice the light in your room, the wrinkle of sheets, the smell of air. Be present as you go through your day, mindful of such details as the mist rising from the orange you peel, the ridges of pattern in the peel's color that fade to yellow near the green nub of stem, and the stem's starlike pattern.

Notice what you notice, take the high points, and write them down in your notebook. Create word sketches of gesture, sound, color, texture. By paying attention to what you notice, you begin to see how the writer in you views the world and relationships. These recorded word pictures validate the world you see and experience. By paying attention and writing what you perceive, you find your own truth, and this is what you will pass on in your writing.

*See Truth Is in the Details, Slow Down, Hunting and Gathering*

## Write from the Senses

The senses provide a physical world for our writing as well as a palette for rich imagery and language. It's through the five senses that we ground our writing in the concrete — the sight, sound, smell, taste, and feel of it — moving out of our heads and into our bodies. Words and descriptions reach out from the page and into the sensory perceptions of the reader and the piece comes to life for him.

Within the realm of the senses are born metaphor and simile. One thing is another; something is like something else. Imagery emerges from the chrysalis of sensuous language and takes wing.

As you write, pause to take a sensory inventory. Close your eyes and breathe in the smell of the place you're writing, listen to its sounds, reach out and feel the textures, taste the air, the wind, the rain. It's not words you are looking for, but, as Beat writer Jack Kerouac put it, "to see the picture better" — the colors, the shapes and textures of it, the way the light falls upon the bricks, the shadows of doorways, the movement of fog over river.

■ Begin writing-practice sessions with "I remember the smell of ... I remember the taste of ... I remember the feel of ... I remember the sound of ... I remember the sight of ..." Focusing on one sense, capture in three or four short sentences the first image that comes to you, collecting specific details as you go. As you put the concluding period on your first paragraph, but before you stop to think of another memory, write "I remember (the sense) ..." again and catch the next image. You may be surprised by the images that appear and the memo-

*The main thing is to immerse ourselves in the material, and reach for the intensity.*
— Anne Rice

| | |
|---|---|
| February 5 | "When I awoke the next morning ... " |
| February 6 | Write about a stranger. |
| February 7 | "Everybody loves the sound of a train in the distance. Everybody thinks it's true." (after Paul Simon) |
| February 8 | Write about a river. |

ries that are evoked, especially if you keep your pen moving and don't stop to try and remember.

Fill a page with four or five short memories, then choose one and do an expanded writing from it, starting with the memory as you first wrote it, or enter the image from another point. Keep the rest of your list for later practice sessions.

You can do these sensory "I remember" exercises again and again; you're almost guaranteed a new set of memories each time. If one image continues to reappear, you can be certain it is one that wants to be written about. Honor it by writing it.

*One of the real tests of writers, especially poets, is how well they write about scents.*

— Diane Ackerman

■ Create pages in your notebook for litanies of smells, tastes, textures, colors, shapes, sounds. Continue to weed out clichés as they sprout. When you come upon one, rework it to make it fresh.

■ Describe a place using only sight, only smell, only sound, only taste, only touch.

■ Take a sensory tour of your bed, your desk, your room, your house, your backyard. Sit with your notebook for a time and write your perceptions like an artist who continues to look from subject to page, sketching in details, then going back for more. ⪷

## Auditioning Words

This is how important words are: Imagine you're the director and you're casting words for your next production. You could say "the plot's the thing" and any old words that tell the story will work just fine. Yes, and imagine Goofy as Richard III, or Miss Piggy as Blanche DuBois. "The difference between the right word and almost the right word is the difference between lightning and a lightning bug," said the great American writer Mark Twain.

Audition your words. Go for better. Don't settle for red when crimson is the word you want. If not crimson, what about carmine, scarlet, garnet. Let a whisper be a murmur, a snuffle, a soft lament.

Read your words out loud and listen for the rhythm, the repeated sounds, the slant rhymes that happen inside as you string (chain, tier, caravan) the words together. Study poetry for its rhythm and musicality. Author and teacher Gary Provost wrote, "Writing is not a visual art. It is a symphony, not an oil painting. It is the shattering, not the glass. It is the ringing, not the bell. The words you write make sounds, and when the sounds satisfy the reader's ear, your writing works."

As you read other writers, notice words and the certain coincidence of words that excite you; write these words in your notebook. Use them in your daily writing practice. Become a connoisseur of words. A wordsmith, honing and crafting the language into art.

*See Wordplay, About Language, Better Verbs*

*Words are, of course, the most powerful drug used by mankind.*
— Rudyard Kipling

| | |
|---|---|
| February 9 | Write about a wild-eyed dream. |
| February 10 | You hear church bells in the distance. |
| February 11 | This is how my heart was broken. |
| February 12 | Write your morning. |

## Self-Sabotage

Sometimes writers undermine their best writing intentions, often without being aware of how they are harming themselves and their writer's spirit. Following is a list of some of the ways you can sabotage yourself and your work.

- Not keeping appointments with yourself to write.
- Allowing others' needs/wants/schedules to interfere with your writing time.
- Allowing people you don't trust to read your writing.
- Comparing your first-draft writing to someone else's finished, published piece.
- Not completing pieces. Stopping when the going gets tough or things get uncomfortable or when you feel stuck.
- Believing there is such a thing as perfect. Perfectionism is the number one enemy of all creative efforts!
- Setting standards too high, making goals too lofty: to write for three hours every day when a half hour is more realistic; setting out to write a novel without knowing any of the basics of the craft; simply starting at chapter one, page one.
- Holding unrealistic expectations: to write a novel in three months; complete a short story in a single setting; write a finished essay in the first draft.
- Believing because a piece is rejected, it isn't good. Or worse, that *you* aren't any good. Taking no for an answer. Letting one person's subjective opinion be the ultimate judgment of a piece.
- Sending out material that isn't ready. Not doing research and sending the right piece to the wrong publisher.
- Believing publication means success.
- Writing and working in a vacuum. You need other writers, other opinions.

Most self-sabotaging behavior comes out of fear — fear of claiming our writer-self, fear of disappointing others or of not getting approval or acceptance, fear of success. "Our deepest fear is not that we are inadequate. Our deepest fear is that we are powerful beyond measure," said South African leader Nelson Mandela. When you begin to honor your writing-self, saying "Yes!" to all you are, self-sabotage will disappear.

*See Top Ten Fears of Writers, Honor Yourself as Writer, Find Support for Your Writing Life*

*If I knew what was going to happen next, I wouldn't be able to write. I wouldn't be interested in writing.*

— Walker Percy

## The Difference between Writing Practice and Journal Writing

Writing practice and journal writing have much in common; however, they are two very different processes. Writing practice is focused, creative writing on a topic; journaling is writing for self-exploration, self-expression, and, often, catharsis. While both might be freewheeling and personal, one can be considered public writing and the other private.

Journal-writing techniques focus on going within, writing feelings, reflections, thoughts, and opinions, and provide a forum for processing emotions that arise from introspection. A journal is a place for recording a life, safekeeping memories, dwelling within, and working through. We write to know and express ourselves.

Writing practice is about finding our voices and telling our stories in a creative way — using the craft of writing and the expressive channels of language, imagery, metaphor. We invent and fictionalize, compress and exaggerate. We employ the tools of the craft: dialogue, setting, point of view, mood. Characters are invited in and booted out without regard to "what really happened." We lie to get at the truth and board flights of fancy that transport us to the outer edges of our imaginations. We practice to express ourselves and to get better at our craft.

This is not to say that journal writing cannot be a creative act. Often imaginative, creative writing is found within the sacred pages of personal journals and can be lifted whole and transplanted into a story, essay, or novel. And, for certain, writing-practice pieces can help us process and heal, lead us inward on

*Everything we learn to write is a stepping stone for the next level of conversation we are capable of having with ourselves.*

— Christina
   Baldwin

| | |
|---|---|
| February 13 | You're moving into a new house; write about the people or person who lived there before you. |
| February 14 | Write about the night sky. |
| February 15 | Write about a brief encounter. |
| February 16 | Someone gave you flowers. |

roads otherwise not taken. Expose us to ourselves.

Journal keeping and writing practice are not at odds with one another. In fact, they complement each other. Within the journal we find evocative topics to rummage through in practice sessions; during writing practice we touch upon tender places that we may want to explore within the private confines of our journals.

Though some writers like to use the same notebook for journaling and writing practice, a separate notebook for each is recommended. This holds back the tendency to journalize during writing practice and to choose the creative over the introspective in the journal. ❧

*I write out of curiosity and bewilderment.*

— William Trevor

## Invoking the Muse

The poet **Friedrich von Schiller** used to keep rotten apples under the lid of his desk, open it, inhale deeply, and compose.

Tea was the stimulant for **Dr. Johnson** and **W. H. Auden**. Johnson was reported to have frequently consumed twenty-five cups at one sitting. **Honoré de Balzac** drank fifty cups of coffee in a day.

**Colette** first picked fleas from her cat, then wrote.

While writing *The Charterhouse of Parma*, **Stendhal** began the day by reading two or three pages of the French civil code.

**Willa Cather** read the Bible.

**Samuel Taylor Coleridge** indulged in two grains of opium before working.

**Alexandre Dumas**, the elder, wrote his nonfiction on rose-colored paper, his fiction on blue, and his poetry on yellow. **Langston Hughes** also used a different kind of paper for each project.

**Rudyard Kipling** insisted on the blackest ink available and fantasized about keeping "an ink-boy to grind me Indian ink."

**Voltaire** used his lover's naked back as a writing desk.

It's said that **Edgar Allen Poe** wrote with his cat on his shoulder.

**T. S. Eliot** preferred writing when he had a head cold.

**Paul West** listened nonstop to a sonatina by Ferruccio Busoni while he wrote *The Place in Flowers Where Pollen Rests*, while **Hart Crane** wrote to Cuban rumbas, Maurice Ravel's *Bolero*, and torch songs.

| | |
|---|---|
| February 17 | Open the box. |
| February 18 | Blue — the color or the emotion. |
| February 19 | Write about a quilt or a blanket. |
| February 20 | Close your eyes. Write about what you see. |
| February 21 | Someone's playing the radio. |

# Ten ^Daily^ Habits That Make a (Good) Writer

1. **Eat Healthfully** — Give your body what it really wants so it can support you. You may think it wants caffeine, sugar, or alcohol, but it really wants broccoli and spinach. Eat healthfully for stamina, good health, and the sensory experience of it. (Notice your carrots when you eat them, their color and crunch. Smell that onion; look closely at its layers and textures.) Eat several small meals throughout the day; begin with a good breakfast.

2. **Be Physical** — Remember when your mother warned you about making faces: "your face could freeze that way." If you're sitting at your desk all hours of the day and night, your whole body could petrify that way. Move it; stretch, exercise, work out. Breathe. It roils the blood and feeds the brain. When you walk, run, bicycle, or swim, you're in touch with the earth (unless you do it in a gym and in that case, GET OUTSIDE). Do it alone so you can pay attention to your body and notice your environment as you glide along.

3. **Laugh Out Loud** — You take big breaths when you laugh out loud. Laughing helps rid the body of toxins. So lighten up. Take a break from work and play with your puppy or your child or your neighbor's child. Look at cartoons; tell a joke; share with friends. Find something funny in the world and let loose belly laughs. Create a playground for the Muse.

4. **Read** — Read as much as you can of the best writers. Read on two levels: one as a reader and one as a writer. Study how other writers use language, how they construct a piece. Notice what you love about certain writers. Try reading aloud (especially poetry) before you write.

5. **Cross-Fertilize** — Experience another art form — music, photography, dance, painting, sculpture, film, theater. Keep open books of art in your writing space, a basketful of postcard art to leaf through. If music distracts you while you write, listen at other times when you can absorb the music and it is not just a background sound. Visit a museum; walk in a sculpture garden. Let other art evoke your own.

6. **Practice Spirituality** — Take time every day (or several times a day) to consciously go to that place you name Sacred — through prayer, meditation, or

*You have to give away your TV, you have to read out loud two hours a day minimum. You have to walk in the hills alone and always carry a notebook.*

— Kate
　Braverman

. . . . . . . . . . . . . . . . . . . . . . . . . . . . . . . . . . . . . . . . . . . . . . . . . . . . . . .

simply being mindful and present in the present. Make time for whatever you do that keeps you in touch with your spiritual self.

7. **Pay Attention** — Notice the quality of light, the heft of air, color of sky, faces, clouds, flowers, garbage, graffiti — all of it. Slow down and pay attention. Stop during your walks and examine a leaf. Read the writing in shop windows. Observe people getting on a bus, the bus driver, the stink of the bus exhaust.

8. **Give Back** — Do something good or kind for someone or the planet. Speak to someone you don't know, smile, help a friend (or a stranger), plant a flower, reuse a paper bag, walk instead of driving. Be generous with whatever you have to give.

*I'm a writer. I don't cook and I don't clean.*
— Dorothy West

9. **Connect with Another Writer** — Meet a writing friend for coffee, write a letter to a writer whose work you admire, make a phone call to a writer friend. Attend a poetry reading, a book signing; take part in a workshop. Write with someone. Go on-line to a writers' chat room, e-mail a poem to a friend.

10. **Write** — Sometime, someplace, every day, honor your writer-self and spend some time writing. ❧

| | |
|---|---|
| February 22 | Write about a tattoo. |
| February 23 | These are the pleasures I have known. |
| February 24 | Once, in the midst of all the recklessness … |
| February 25 | "By the sea, beneath the yellow and sagging moon." (after Walt Whitman) |

## Who Reads Your Writing

Exposing your writing, especially the raw, uncooked stuff of writing practice, can be risky. Handing over a notebook filled with the shaggy evidence of practice sessions to someone who doesn't understand the purpose of practice, or someone who believes it is in your best interest to be critiqued, may not be wise. In fact, even if you're not easily embarrassed, handing over your notebook to anyone is probably not a good choice.

*You're the first audience to your work, and the most important audience.*

— Gloria Naylor

Pieces written during practice sessions are not meant for critique. They're not ready yet. Some of them may never be.

Only after you've rewritten, edited, polished, and generally cleaned up a piece will you want to ask for critique. Even then, family and friends are seldom the best audience. They may feel as if they have to criticize the writing, but they don't know what to criticize (Are you sure you want to name your character Maude? Should this be a comma or a semicolon?); they may criticize you rather than the writing (You never were very good at grammar); or they may think any criticism will hurt your feelings and gush with false accolades (Gosh, honey, this is just great. Have you thought of sending it to *The New Yorker?*). Better to ask someone you can trust — preferably another writer whose work you respect and whom you respect as a person, too.

A good read-and-critique group where you are a regular participant is best. Find one made up of writers at your same level of experience and just beyond, either a peer group or with an instructor with whom you're comfortable. If you can't find listings for such groups via local publications or on the Internet, start your own.

*See How to Start a Writing-Practice Group, Find Your Tribe, Find Support for Your Writing Life*

## Snowbound
### (or The Serendipitous Effects of Bad Weather on a Good Writer)

There's six feet of new snow and outside your window a gauzy shroud of white obliterates any horizon.

Or, it's been raining since eight o'clock last night and it's still coming down. You now understand deluge, monsoon, and torrent.

Or, some cosmic cook has over-seasoned the soup and the fog is as thick as bouillabaisse.

Let's just say that, for whatever reason, and through forces outside your control, you're homebound for the day. Consider this a gift. You've been given a writing day, free and clear.

This is a day for snugging in. Think of words like *warm, fuzzy, cozy*. Brew up some cocoa; hot, spiced tea; coffee with warmed milk. A few cookies or buttered toast won't go astray. Build a crackling fire or, lacking a fireplace, encircle your nest with candles. Get your notebook, your favorite pen, and settle in.

Warm up with a five-minute writing (topic: Write about a small thing), then maybe a ten-minute writing, (topic: You are in a garden). Refresh your coffee or tea, give the fire a poke, and encamp yourself again. Release all constraints of time and begin another writing session. Continue writing one of the pieces you've already begun, or start fresh (topic: "It was Monday morning"). Instead of stopping after fifteen or twenty minutes, keep going. When you come to what might be a stopping place, rather than a period, put a comma and keep writing. Or, begin again with a connector such as "then" or "however" or "instead of" or "but" and allow the pen to begin its meanderings anew. Write as long

| | |
|---|---|
| February 26 | The last time. |
| February 27 | Write about fireworks. |
| February 28 | What if … |
| February 29 | Write about a balcony. |

as you want. Let this be a leisurely session; there's no schedule to keep, nothing to do instead of write.

Stay warm. Keep writing. Here are a few more topics, just in case you need them.

- Write about a mirror.
- Write a February memory.
- "After all, it wasn't what she expected."
- This is not about ...
- One Friday night.

P.S. It doesn't have to be snowing or raining or foggy for you to give yourself a homebound day. Simply take one. It will be good for any old winter doldrums that might have crept in. 🐦

*The trick is to make time — not to steal it — and produce fiction.*

— Bernard Malamud

# MARCH

"As I write I create myself
again and again."

—Joy Harjo

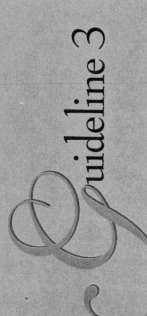

Guideline 3

## Don't Judge Your Writing

When writing in real time you're bound to be clumsy sometimes; to repeat yourself; change names; switch gender, tense, or even point of view. To use common words and commit clichés. Never mind. Just keep writing. Remember, you're not editing or revising as you write, or considering what might be a better way to express yourself. What gets written in writing practice is the roughest of rough drafts — writing that is pouring directly from the intuitive, too fragile and raw for judgments. Especially your own because, more likely than not, you are your own harshest critic. As Eleanor Roosevelt said, "No one can do to me what I have not already done to myself."

When writing in a group with other writing practitioners, don't compare, analyze, or criticize this bare, uncooked stuff. Or compare your unfinished, first drafts with the finished, published work of other writers. There comes a time to judge your writing and to ask for critique from others, but it is not during writing practice.

All this may be easier said than done. We tend to rush to judgment, to expect better from ourselves no matter how good or fresh or alive our writing may be. "Nothing you write, if you hope to be any good, will ever come out as you first hoped," said playwright Lillian Hellman. Remember to be your own best friend — nonjudgmental, accepting, tolerant, loving, kind, and patient. And remember to laugh sometimes. At yourself and your writing.

## Perfectionism

Perfectionism is an ugly thing, all stiff and rigid with pursed lips and beady little eyes. No one likes perfectionism. It comes from a stingy, mean-spirited place and serves no purpose except to make us feel terrible about ourselves and anything we create.

Perfectionism causes us to hold our pens too tight and reject words and ideas before we get them down. If we do evade perfectionism temporarily, when it finds us again, it orders us to cross out, erase, rewrite anything we have written in its absence.

Perfectionism would have God recast every sunset and chide Mother Nature for her choice of colors. If everything were left up to perfectionism, nothing would exist.

You won't hear perfectionism say, "Ah, this is good." Its entire vocabulary begins with *n* words: No, Not, Never.

Poet William Stafford said, "What one has written is not to be defended or valued, but abandoned: others must decide significance and value."

Knowing perfect does not exist, or believing that creations (including ourselves) are perfect in their imperfections, lets us make a thing as good as we can, raising to the highest level our abilities allow that which we have created. Then we are able to call it complete, release it, and move on.

*See How to Tell When the Critic Is Present*

*A perfect poem is impossible. Once it had been written, the world would end.*

— Robert Graves

---

Writing Topics

| | |
|---|---|
| March 1 | Write about hair. |
| March 2 | This much is known … |
| March 3 | You see a shooting star. |
| March 4 | "At 5 in the afternoon." (after Federico García Lorca) |
| March 5 | What are you waiting for? |

## TIP
### OF THE MONTH

*Work with all your intelligence and love. Work freely and rollickingly as though you were talking to a friend who loves you. Mentally (at least three or four times a day) thumb your nose at all the know-it-alls, jeerers, critics, doubters.*

— Brenda Ueland

## Top Ten Fears of Writers

A survey of regular writing practitioners showed these as the top ten fears of practicing the craft. How do your fears compare?

1. that I'm not good enough; that my writing is mediocre or bad
2. that my work is worthless, boring, drivel, not clever; that I have nothing interesting to say
3. that I won't follow through or complete anything
4. that I'll get stuck and nothing will come out
5. that I'll never learn the craft of writing
6. that I'll appear stupid or foolish; afraid of what people will think
7. that I'll hurt someone
8. that I'm a fake, lying, not telling the truth
9. that it's a waste of time

A tie for 10:

10. that it's been done or said before, better
10. that I won't get published

## Top Ten Joys of Writers

Those same writers, when asked to list their top ten joys about writing, came up with the following list. A number of ties emerged; we've included them all.

1. expressed many ways: the feeling of completeness, of being in sync with the universe, being present in the now, centered, peaceful, calm, being with myself
2. feeling that I entertained the reader, made people laugh, touched someone
3. the feeling of being creative, "in the groove," *being* an artist
3. telling a story, creating characters, plots
4. connecting with others
4. playing with words, using language
4. having an audience, having other people read or hear my writing
5. expressing myself, putting myself on paper, recording my thoughts
5. being with other writers
6. finding out about myself
6. producing something
7. being published
7. finishing, the feeling of having written
7. leaving a legacy, making a mark on the world
8. becoming a more discerning reader
9. finding out I'm good, that there is promise
10. the surprises, finding out what happens

*It's a great relief to me to know that I can actually be creative and be happy at the same time.*

— James W. Hall

| March 6 | Write about someone who left. |
| March 7 | Write about a time you won, Big. |
| March 8 | Night. |
| March 9 | Write about a secret revealed. |
| March 10 | Give me a moon story. |
| March 11 | "You have stayed too long." |

## How to Tell When the Editor Is Present

The editor is the voice that makes you cross out words, rifle through the dictionary, double-check the name of a mountain, and call information for the area code for Portland. Editors are important, but like holding off wearing your white shoes until after Memorial Day, there's a right time for everything.

These quotes from writing practitioners are sure signs the editor is present.

*You must be unintimidated by your own thoughts because if you write with someone looking over your shoulder, you'll never write.*

*— Nikki Giovanni*

"I fuss over a single word much too long, instead of just getting the 'mess' on paper first. Then I lose the momentum of the original idea that got me writing and abandon it altogether."     — Steve Montgomery, San Diego

"I stop to read every sentence as I write it rather than just getting the words down."     — Margo Miller, San Diego

"I just sit and stare at the notebook or computer. Nothing comes out. I let choosing one word stop me for an hour from writing anything else."

— anonymous

"Whenever the critic stops to take a drink of water I hear the editor say, 'Don't you think we could say that a little more succinctly?'"

— James Spring,
aboard his boat, San Diego Harbor

"Black squiggly ink blotches appear all over my page."

— Amy Wallen, Del Mar

"I can tell the editor is present when there are more cross outs than words."

— Michelle Murphy Zive, La Mesa

"I get hung up on a word instead of letting the pen move."

— Rosalie Newberg, El Cajon

"Fixation on a single paragraph or sentence and going over and over the same stuff/words."     — Christy Hightower, La Jolla

If you experience these telltale signs of Editor-at-Work, especially in practice or when you're writing first drafts, consider sending her out for coffee while you put in your practice time.

## False Starts

It may happen during any given practice session. You're on a roll with two or three sentences of what feels pretty good, when you're suddenly stopped dead, absolutely unable to continue. Or, those two or three roiling sentences cool down to a thin trickle, finally petering out into a desert of bony, dry words. In writing practice, we call this a false start. The image gives out, or you know you've started something you can't sustain. Or two or three sentences in and you're already boring yourself. These false starts may happen more than once on any given topic. When this occurs, simply drop down a line or two, and start again until you find your groove. Sometimes it may be as simple as restating one of the lines you've already written, coming at it from a slightly different angle or entering through another door. Especially if the image is compelling.

However, it's possible to have a whole day of false starts when you just can't get into anything. When this happens, it could be that your mind is away on other business and hasn't joined you at the desk, or the stress of your "other" life is keeping you from being present with your writing. Try bringing yourself to the present by taking a few deep breaths and settling into your chair with a grounding meditation, then start your writing practice again. Use the same topic, or choose another. I always have extra topics stashed away in my notebook. Or, start your writing with "I remember . . ." or "I think . . ." or "This morning . . ." and just follow your pen.

Caution: The urge to avoid a path because it's scary or feels out of control isn't the same as a false start.

*See Take Risks, Avoiding the Truth*

*Finding the stories is not the hard part. Writing them down is.*

— E. Annie Proulx

| March 12 | Write about stealing something. |
| March 13 | Write about a longing. |
| March 14 | Write about a justifiable sin. |
| March 15 | "If I had my way . . ." |
| March 16 | Write about small injuries. |
| March 17 | On the eve of the funeral. |

## Truth Is in the Details

Details, truthfully rendered, bring your writing to life and create connection points for the reader. It is from these connection points — oh, a red damask tablecloth with a gravy stain … the maître d' with a mole above his lip where a thick, black hair protrudes … the woman with her "eyes as dark as wet black currants" — that a world emerges. Using the writer's specific details as a runway, the reader's imagination can soar into the universe of the story.

*Caress the detail, the divine detail.*

— Vladimir Nabokov

Single, telling details skillfully wrought relate more about a character or a place than a thousand more general aspects. "She would never go to California; she needed to stay in a place where she knew the names of the trees." "At 48, she's had only one serious relationship in her life and has never owned her own washer and dryer."

As you write, reach out to grab the tail of a detail — the color of sky, smell of air, objects within your sight. Search the nooks and crannies of your image for specifics. Use your senses to give heft and texture to the details.

Of course, it is possible to use too many details, bogging down the forward motion of the story with details of the room where it takes place. Go ahead and put them in as they come to you in the first draft. As you rewrite, you'll trim, edit, and hone, keeping the strongest, the most telling details for the current piece and tossing the others, or storing them in the pantry of your notebook for another stew.

Another powerful effect of details is in giving things their names. When you name things, you are telling the truth. The Missouri River. The Sangre de Cristo Mountains. The chinook blowing in off the northwestern Pacific. Thursday. April. Whippoorwill. Billy's Lunch Counter.

"Specificity is generosity," someone once said. Be a generous writer; give details as if they were gifts — from you to the reader.

*See Pay Attention, Guideline 9 — Write Accurate Details*

## Writers on Reading

**Michael Dorris** wrote "reading anything that moves you, disturbs you, thrills you is a path into the great swirl of humanity, past, present, and future."

**Philip Roth** reported that he reads all the time when he's working. He said it's a way to keep the circuits open and to think about the work while getting a little rest from the work at hand.

**Raymond Carver** said he thought all writers — especially young writers — would want to read anything they can get their hands on. He also said that finally, though, a young writer must choose between being a writer or a reader.

For **Ursula Hegi**, reading and rebellion were closely linked during her early teen years.

**Gretel Ehrlich** said reading was an antidote for a "strongly felt cerebral loneliness." She described it as a passage out of the protective constraints prescribed for us by our parents and society.

Reading means questioning, said **J. D. McClatchy** and "sensing that what you read is unfinished until it is completed in the self."

**Kathleen Norris** remarked that just the knowledge that a good book waited at the end of a long day made that day happier.

**Rose Macaulay** suggested there is only one hour in the day that is more pleasurable than the hour spent in bed with a book before going to sleep. It is "the hour spent in bed with a book after being called in the morning."

| | |
|---|---|
| March 18 | Write about promises that were broken. |
| March 19 | You're in the backseat of a taxi. |
| March 20 | This is a map to where I live. |
| March 21 | Write about a fortune-teller. |
| March 22 | Write about taking the long way around. |

## About Language

Language is more than words. Language is music and rhythm; it is sound, rhyme, and sibilance; it is texture and layers. Art and graffiti. Language is attitude and place, geography and history. Language is family and what you heard at the kitchen table and on the back porch, muffled behind closed doors and shouted up from stairwells. Language is what you do with words and it is the silence between the words.

It is impossible, we sometimes think, to convey what we feel or what we want to express in words, those "small shapes in the gorgeous chaos of the world." Yet, other times, it is almost as if we are tracing with our pen words that are already in place, near-perfect and exact.

" … To say what you want to say, you must create another language and nourish it for years and years with what you have loved, with what you have lost, with what you will never find again," wrote poet George Seferis.

How to find and claim your own language:

■ Write that which you heard around your childhood kitchen table, in your grandmother's house, when family gathered and stories were told. Write from "I remember … " prompts to generate images.

■ Write stream of consciousness, allowing language that comes from the deep, unconscious place to take shape on your page. Read aloud what you've written to hear the language of your intuitive voice; listen for words, rhythms, sounds. "There is a sense in sounds beyond their meaning," said poet Wallace Stevens.

■ List five scents, sounds, emotions, tastes, textures, things you see. Then create similes (something is like something else) for each item. Do it quickly without thinking too hard. Avoid the easy cliché. Your "something else" will speak in your own language.

■ Study authors you love to read and whose language resonates with you. Copy whole passages of their writing into your notebook so you sense the physicality of their language. When you read phrases that make you catch your breath, write them down. Use them as writing prompts for practice sessions.

■ Write monologues from the point of view of yourself in different photographs, either real pictures or those you imagine. Give the you in the photo a

*The language still strikes me as a miracle, a thing the deepest mind adores. At its best, when you lose your arrogance and are least selfish, it can sing back to you almost as a disembodied friend.*

— Barry Hannah

voice on the page, writing in the first person. Begin with "In this one I am … " or simply begin with the first thought that comes.

■ Let music suggest language. Listen to different types of music, from big symphonies to acoustical guitar — classical, jazz, rock, rap, ethnic and world music, and write the language you hear.

■ As you read through newspapers or magazines, notice which photographs draw your attention. There is something in these particular pictures that is speaking in your language. Tear out these photos (not the accompanying story or article) and keep them in a folder. As a writing-practice exercise, pull one of the pictures and write from it — a monologue from an individual, a dialogue between two or more people, or make up a story about the subjects. Look long at the image before you begin to "hear" the language that is being spoken.

■ Writing an unsent letter allows you to communicate what you want or need to say to someone in language you might not be able to use in person. For example, you can write your anger at a person who you would never be able to confront or you can say good-bye to someone you might not have had closure with, even someone who has died. Such letters use the language of our emotions. In your notebook, make a list of people to whom you want to write unsent letters. Now choose someone from the list and write the letter. Not only will you discover the language of your heart, writing such letters can be a very healing experience.

■ "Language alone protects us from the scariness of things with no name," said Nobel laureate Toni Morrison. Use the language of your fears, give voice to your terrors, call them up in the night and name them. Do this too with your joys and your pleasures. Write in the language of your prayers. ❧

*See Wordplay, Auditioning Words, Better Verbs*

*Developing a language of one's own, with its distinct colors and nuances, with maps and charts and images that voice the self, takes a long time. It is the writer's lifelong work.*

— Burghild Nina Holzer

| | |
|---|---|
| March 23 | "I remember how it was to drive in gravel." (after Theodore Roethke) |
| March 24 | Write about getting caught in the act. |
| March 25 | Write what you didn't do. |
| March 26 | There were signs and signals. |

## What to Expect after a Practice Session

This is what one writer said about the act of writing: The blank sheet of paper terrified him; the actual placing of words on the page was agonizing; but what he loved, and perhaps why he even did the thing, was what he got afterward — the feeling of having written.

Whatever your process and however you approach the act of writing, the following is what you might expect to experience after a practice session.

- commingled feelings of being spent and being exhilarated
- maybe a little in awe of your own writing and the images that appeared during the session
- some self-righteousness and pride in having done the thing
- disappointment or letdown, especially on one of those "frog-kissing" days
- a little ungrounded, off balance; after all, you've just performed a creative high-wire act, treading that thin strand between conscious and subconscious

Take a few good, deep breaths. Notice your surroundings; feel your feet on the floor, your bottom in the chair, your hands on the table or desk or in your lap. Feel good about yourself, pat yourself on the back. Regardless of how the writing went today, you suited up and showed up and did the work.

*There's a suspense in the process of writing which I've learned to be both charmed and faintly, decently — terrified by.*

*— John Barth*

## Café Writing

Think of Paris. Henry Miller and Lawrence Durrell at *La Coupole*, Simone de Beauvoir and Jean-Paul Sartre at the *Flore*, Djuna Barnes and Saul Bellow at *Cafe de la Mare*. Think of Ernest Hemingway at *Le Deux Maggots* writing of a pretty girl "with a face as fresh as a newly minted coin if they minted coins in smooth flesh with rain-freshened skin."

Cafés have always presented writers a warm and friendly place for work and companionship. And not just in Paris. In San Francisco's Caffe Trieste, just around the corner from Lawrence Ferlinghetti's City Lights Book Store, contingents of Beats gathered. And in *Writing Down the Bones*, you can follow Natalie Goldberg's trail in cafés from Taos to St. Paul.

Cafés offer writers ambience and aroma, conversation and coffee, often set against a background of good music you can listen to or not. The stimulation of sounds and smells and contained hubbub surfs the periphery of your senses while you lean into your notebook and write about somewhere else.

Morning, afternoon, evening — choose a time and take your notebook to your favorite café for a writing-practice session. If you don't have a favorite place, make pilgrimages to several, finding one where you can settle in and make yourself comfortable. Plan to stay for an hour or an afternoon. Do timed writings, or let yourself write as long as you want. Write from a topic, then go back in and open the doors you have created. *(See Doors and Windows.)*

Use your surroundings to add seasoning to your writing — bits of an overheard conversation here (that you eavesdrop on, oh so nonchalantly), a character sketch there (based on that very interesting man with the fedora who sits by

| March 27 | Write about memories underfoot. |
| March 28 | "The last time I saw _____ ," |
| March 29 | Write about something astonishing. |
| March 30 | "So, these were my friends … " (after John Balaban) |
| March 31 | Every morning … |

the window reading Proust). Incorporate the art, the music, the light that transforms the glass bottles of flavoring into a shelf of decanted rainbows — fold all these café morsels into your writing like chocolate chips into cookie dough. Yum.

If you always go to the same café, just for a change, try some place new where the chairs aren't so familiar and the *barrista* doesn't know your favorite drink. Change creates a tension that can inform your writing in subtle ways, just as does the very essence of the café.

*I am what is around me.*

— Wallace Stevens

Suggested topics:

- Write about the taste of sorrow.
- These are the things I saved.
- Write about what is true at first light and a lie by noon. (after Hemingway)
- "I stand between quiet and silence." (after Lizzie Wann)
- Write about a small rebellion
- Write about being in bad company.

# April

"If we had to say what writing is,
we would define it essentially
as an act of courage."

—Cynthia Ozick

Guideline 4

## Let Your Writing Find Its Own Form

Form will come organically out of what you write. You don't have to have a beginning, middle, and end for what you write in practice sessions. In fact, if you are writing in short fifteen- or twenty-minute sessions, it will be difficult to create such a structure. Nor does what you write have to fit into some container labeled story or essay or poem. If you attempt to force form, you may miss revelations that might otherwise appear. Letting go of any preconceived ideas of what you want to write will set free a tremendous energy to write what wants to be written.

During any given practice session, you may write an essay, a poem, bits and pieces of a story, dialogue, fragments, a character sketch, or something more akin to a journal entry. Don't try to control your writing or make your writing into anything specific, just let it flow the way it wants. Like water following the path of least resistance, the real, authentic stuff will find its own way. Then, as you move through the exercise, a form will emerge. What began as the cusp of a memory may evolve into a prose poem. A character sketch is suddenly a scene with two characters in dialogue and one of them is pretty mad. A piece on what you learned in high school reads like the nub of a personal narrative.

"One may do *anything*," the poet Rainer Maria Rilke told us. "This alone corresponds to the whole breadth life has."

## The Effects of Writing Practice

If becoming a better writer were the only benefit of writing practice, it would be enough. But, like so many other practices, what you get is often a whole lot more than you signed up for. Call them bonuses, rewards, extras, gifts, fringe benefits, or dividends, these are the promises inherent in writing practice.

- Daily writing-practice sessions will improve your writing.
- Writing will come easier and be less forced.
- You'll take more risks in your writing.
- You'll become less self-conscious; your writing will be looser, freer.
- You'll learn your rhythms as a writer, to trust your ups and downs.
- You'll find out what matters to you as a writer and what you want to write about.
- You'll discover your secrets and glimpse your shadows.
- You'll have an opportunity to grieve what needs to be grieved, and to heal.
- You'll feel good about yourself as writer and experience increased self-esteem.
- You'll fill notebooks, which may mean the beginnings, middles, and endings of some projects you didn't even know you wanted to write.

*You develop a style from writing a lot.*

— Kurt Vonnegut

The effects of daily writing practice may not come immediately and they may be subtle in their appearance, but keep in mind there are those who believe the tiny flutter of a butterfly's wings in China creates hurricanes off the coast of Mexico.

Writing Topics

| | |
|---|---|
| April 1 | You're in a grocery store. |
| April 2 | "I would like to make an exchange." |
| April 3 | Write about your mother's cooking. |
| April 4 | It was a rainy day. |

## TIP
### OF THE MONTH

*You need to trust your-self, especially on a first draft, where amid the anxiety and self-doubt, there should be a real sense of your imagination and your memories walking and woolgather-ing, tramping the hills, romping all over the place. Trust them. Don't look at your feet to see if you are doing it right. Just dance.*

— Anne Lamott

## Go Deeper

Sometimes a writer skates on top of a subject. Or tap-dances around it. The writing is glib and clever and absolutely without a trace of depth. Or maybe the writing is nice, like the sweet woman who wears pale flowered dresses and smiles no matter what. No one can find fault with her; it's just that she's so, well, nice. But somehow you don't quite trust her because you don't believe she's being honest. So it is when you hold back from a subject that has deeper meaning for you. You don't trust yourself, so you don't trust your writing.

You may be able to write the facts of the subject: a father's death, a lover's parting, a fire, a flood, a terrible accident, childhood experi-ences related as if they happened to someone else. But you are afraid of the emotions that glide along on the underside of the facts like shadows beneath the ice.

If you are to write the truth, you must go beneath the surface into deeper, often darker waters where the light wavers and breathing is a matter of mindfulness.

"Often the writing process is filled with a sense of jeopardy," said mystery writer Sue Grafton. Going to these deep and scary places takes courage. Novelist and short story writer Kate Braverman told of a time she spent the night curled in the fetal position beneath her desk because of what she knew she must write, but she got up the next morning and continued writing. By writing the truth of your feelings, you get to feel them, and, once felt, you can begin to heal.

To go deeper in your writing:

■ After you have written a certain passage that holds emotion for you, ask yourself how you feel. If you're writing fiction, ask how the character feels. Take a deep breath and feel the emotion, then write what you felt. Never mind if you write clichés, you can always rewrite with fresher images. For now, just get it down.

■ Instead of putting a period at the end of a sentence, put a comma and continue writing. Follow the last word with another specific image that takes the writing further, then do it again and again with each image building to a more powerful effect. For example, the Kate Braverman quote on page 128: "... You build a novel the same way you do a pyramid. One word, one stone at a time, underneath a full moon when the fingers bleed."

Using the comma rather than the period lets the words carry you deeper and deeper into the original image, like this example from writer David Cohen. "Underneath it all, as it baked in the summer heat, as it peeled in the cool dawns of autumn, as it splintered in winter's chill, was tormented with spring rains, equally at the mercy of Nature's unrelenting changes and the shifting fads and festering detritus of the human world. ..."

■ If you stopped because you ran out of time, take more time. Or return to the piece in the next session and begin where you left off. Don't change the subject.
■ In rereading if you notice a place where you pulled your punch, go back in and take off from just before the feint.
■ Close your eyes and envision your face or your body, or that of the character you're writing. Write what you see.
■ Write the sounds of the feeling. Or its colors. Feel the air that surrounds the emotion.
■ Write through your tears. If you begin to cry, don't try to stop it, and don't stop writing either. Let your tears fall on your page and smear your ink and mess up your writing. Remember what the poet Robert Frost said: "No tears for the writer, no tears for the reader." ❧

*See Being Vulnerable on the Page, Take Risks, Breathe, Slow Down*

*Follow your image as far as you can. Push yourself.*
— Nikki Giovanni

| April 5 | Write about eating a meal. |
| April 6 | Write what you'll miss when you die. |
| April 7 | Write about a town you passed through. |
| April 8 | Write about your father's hands. |
| April 9 | You're asleep. You're not at home. |

## Places to Practice

To say cafés may be redundant, but nevertheless, cafés top the list of favorite places to write. The ambience of sensory ambrosia plus the sweet quintessence of time set aside for good and important things make cafés and writing soulmates.

■ Take all that mellow ambience of a café, turn it inside out with bright lights, (probably fluorescent); gurgling, whooshing, thumping noises; the stink of dirty clothes, soap, and bleach; lint-filled air guaranteed to make you sneeze; time ticking away, quarter by quarter; and furrow-browed folks focused on mundane and necessary chores and you've got the Laundromat. A completely different sensory experience and a stimulating place for writing practice. If you have to be there anyhow, what the heck, use it. Use it all.

■ Parks and picnic areas and spaces that are green and lush and open to the sky make natural settings for writing. Sun shining or hidden by clouds, a little hot, too cool? Never mind. Take a walk, take your shoes off, take the time to lie back on the grass and write. And just because you're in the green and blue open spaces, doesn't mean you have to write pastoral. Often the opposite of where we find ourselves is what we write, as the globe-trotting Ernest Hemingway said, writing of Michigan while hunched over café au lait in a Parisian café.

■ Libraries and bookstores (if they offer tables and chairs for lingering book lovers, as many do these days, complete with cafés). Who knows what thoughts or ideas or images or surprising and delicious phrases might find their way into your writing just by sharing the same literary aerie with all those books?

■ Bus depots, train stations, airports, and other way stations where travelers come and go, but you stay in one place and observe them, picking up the buzz of motion and letting its vibration inform your writing.

■ Better still, get aboard that bus headed for the next town over, or hop an outbound train. Take the trolley to the end of the line, hail a taxi for a ten- or twenty-minute ride, or grab some other mode of public transportation (in our town we have romantic horse-and-carriages for hire; pedicabs peddled by sturdy young men with great smiles and muscled calves; short-run trams in all the tourist spots; and a harborful of water taxis, cruise boats, and ferries). You write

*I feel that art has something to do with the achievement of stillness in the midst of chaos. A stillness which characterizes prayer, too, and the eye of the storm.*

— Saul Bellow

while they drive, and let yourself be transported to somewhere else, both in body and writer's spirit.

■ Diners, lunch counters, delis, and coffee shops. You may have to keep buying something to justify your counter space, but the milieu and its accompanying sounds, smells, and flavors can add as much spice to your writing as the Poupon. Never mind the corned beef stains. Leave a big tip.

■ Bars, lounges, joints, and dives. If it's not too dark and the music is good, go ahead. Use the sharp click-clack of pool balls to accent your writing, the hovering blue haze and beer breath of the place. But remember this: unlike genies, the Muse doesn't live in a bottle.

■ Your bed, with pillows piled high behind you, maybe one on your lap to support your notebook, a steamy cup of hot coffee, mint tea, or cocoa within easy reach on the nightstand where a candle dances and a sweet bouquet reminds you that you are loved (even if you did buy it for yourself). Try this practice location first thing in the morning while sleep still clings to your consciousness, or at night before you slide down into dreamy repose. Especially recommended in the midst of some rainy day just before or after you treat yourself to a lovely nap.

■ Keep your notebook with you in your car, and as you're going from here to there, and if it's a beautiful day, take a detour. Park at some fine lookout over a river or above the city or along a stretch of white-sand beach. Slide on over to the passenger side where you've got some elbow room, roll the window down, put your feet up, lean back, and write. Ah, that's better. ❧

*You write by sitting down and writing.*

— Bernard Malamud

| April 10 | "I still don't know … " |
| April 11 | Write about a body part. |
| April 12 | Dubious intentions. |
| April 13 | Write about a time you changed your mind. |
| April 14 | Write about slumming. |

## Doors and Windows

Each piece you write will have doors to open and windows to look through. Like exploring a house, these openings reveal more of the place, what it's made of, how it's built, and the geography of the thing. Going through these doors and looking out these windows (or into them) provides the writer an opportunity for layering, creating texture and depth. When you reread your writing, make notes of these doors and windows. Later, in your rewriting, enter them and follow their passageways and openings.

■ Let's say you're writing about a character who has dreams and fantasies. Rather than just ending the sentence in that vague place — "she had dreams at night" — open the door into the dreams and lay them out for the reader, like taking dresses out of the closet and spreading them across the bed.

■ If being in a place reminds a character of her grandmother's house, go through that door and into a memory of the grandmother's house and something that happened there. The memory should not be random, however, but relate somehow to what is happening to the character now.

■ Describing that night twelve years ago as the most romantic night of your life is bland and meaningless until you pull back the blinds and bring the night into view with specific details of what made it romantic: the setting, the lighting, the way she leaned her head against your shoulder as you danced to "Begin the Beguine" and you could smell the honeysuckle scent of her skin.

■ If a character imagines the kind of woman her ex-lover is with now, describe that woman: bleached hair and long legs and shoes with too many straps, and what the two of them might be doing together now — driving down the coast of California with its palm trees and frothing ocean, with the convertible top down and her hair blowing behind her like a flag of victory.

*See Go Deeper, Rereading Your Practice Pages, Revising*

## Writing Positions

### Standers

Ernest Hemingway
Thomas Wolfe
Virginia Woolf
Lewis Carroll

### Lie-ers Down

Robert Louis Stevenson
Mark Twain
Truman Capote
Dame Edith Sitwell
  (in an open coffin)

### Bathtub Soakers

Benjamin Franklin
Edmond Rostand
Diane Ackerman

### Writers in the Nude

Victor Hugo
Benjamin Franklin
D. H. Lawrence

### Cigar Smokers (among others)

George Sand
Amy Lowell
Mark Twain — 40 a day

### After a Long Walk-ers

Henry David Thoreau
Isaac Bashevis Singer
  (40–60 blocks every morning)
Wallace Stevens
Brenda Ueland
William Wordsworth
John Clare
Carl Sandburg (20 miles a day)
Charles Dickens (20–30 miles a day)

The Writing Life

| | |
|---|---|
| April 15 | These are the things women don't know about love. |
| April 16 | Write about falling from grace. |
| April 17 | Write about what's under your house. |
| April 18 | Just beyond the edge of the woods. |

# When Your Writing Bores Even You

Boring writing happens when writers (a) get lazy, (b) keep treading the same old territory, (c) hold back, (d) play safe, or (e) get too comfortable. Here are some symptoms and antidotes.

**A. Lazy Writers** — Their verbs graze on the hillside like fat cows and their nouns are like cornmeal mush. Their color palette is a six-pack of crayons and the only textures they mention are soft or hard. Their dialogue would make *Leave It to Beaver* sound clever and they've set new records for "number of clichés in one paragraph." They ignore doors that might be opened and never look out any windows.

## Antidote

Play word games, experiment with language, audition words. Use the thesaurus, appropriate a set of paint chips from Home Depot and study the names of colors, take sensory inventories, practice dialogue, eavesdrop on conversations, read Raymond Carver, Pam Houston, Don DeLillo, Lorrie Moore. Reread your work and mark doors and windows. Open and enter during writing-practice exercises.

**B. Same Old Territory** — Everybody in the group sighs when it's this writer's turn to read. We've all heard this story before. And before that and before that. Like the line from the old Herman and the Hermits song "I'm Henry the First, I am," *Second verse/same as the first*; it's another rewrite of the same interminable scene with only a few words changed, or it's another retread of the same story about the same characters singing the same tune. Boring!

## Antidote

Free-write using the writing-practice prompts, writing only new material for the next month. No rewriting or editing allowed! Ban those characters from any further appearances in any stories from now on. Send them to the Retirement Home for Overused Characters. Flip everything: gender, age, profession, politics, hair color, diction, intelligence, geography, sexual preferences. Everything.

**C. Holding Back** — When vague words like "terrible," "difficult," and "painful" make regular appearances, or when clichés like "brokenhearted," "sobbing like a child," or "flew into a rage" are used to describe feelings, you can be fairly certain the writer is holding back. It's hard to care about people or characters who are held at arm's length by abstract words and hackneyed phrases. Readers want the real stuff: the truth.

## Antidote

Ask what was it *exactly* that made something terrible? In what ways was it difficult? What did the pain feel like? Use concrete details and specific images. Use words that describe the terrible, difficult, painful. Write through the cliché with a fresh simile or metaphor. Ask what a broken heart feels like, looks like. What other body parts are affected and how? Find fresh images. Go to your own experience, bring to mind a memory of a time you were brokenhearted, when you sobbed like a child, when you flew into a rage: describe your behavior and your feelings. Take the time to stay with the feeling and write down what you experience.

D. **Playing Safe** — Safe writing is about as exciting as the seventh inning stretch at a bush league ball game when the score is 13-0, visitor's favor. No wonder we're all yawning. Nothing's at stake here. So the cleanup batter hit a foul and broke his bat? Who cares. So their team's winning pitcher gets relieved by the kid up from the sagebrush league. Are we staying for the rest of the game or are we going across the street for a beer?

## Antidote

Write what matters. Be a passionate writer. Don't waste time writing about anything you don't care about. Also, for a reader to be involved in what she's reading, something must be at stake. There must be some kind of tension in the

*... perhaps the most important thing we can ever do in our lives is find a way to keep the wild — both the wild inside and the wild outside us — and tap into it.*

—Anne Rivers Siddons

| April 19 | Write about a time you did something you didn't want to do. |
| April 20 | Write about meeting someone for the first time. |
| April 21 | Something seemed different. |
| April 22 | This is not about ... |

writing to keep the reader's attention. Crank up the heat, put some obstacles in the way of your characters. "Writing is not like parenting," said writer Romelda Shaffer. "Torment, confusion, obstacles, and catastrophes are good things."

When a writer is playing safe, you can bet the censor or critic is somewhere nearby.

**E. Too Comfortable** — The writing is humming along. Show up at writing practice every day, same time, no problems. Writing is easy, four, five pages a day, meeting those goals. Found a genre that works, a groove that fits. Know how to play those plots and story lines, can write a poem on a dime; no surprises, no hassles. This writing business: easy pie.

### Antidote

Just like the antidote for "playing safe," this writer needs to create some tension, crank up the heat, experience a little confusion. Recommended: change the time and place of the daily writing practice. Raise the bar to more pages every day. Switch genres, try something new. Don't fit so easily in the groove, feel the bumps and ridges, the sharp edge. Let your writing surprise you, keep you awake at night. If a writer is too comfortable, you can bet there aren't any risks being taken. No risks = boring writing.

"Beware of creating tedium!" said the prodigious Anthony Trollope. "I know no guard against this so likely to be effective as the feeling of the writer himself. When once the sense that the thing is becoming long has grown upon him, he may be sure that it will grow upon his readers." ❧

*See Try Out Ideas, Fresh Images and How to Find Them, Imagination and Other Surprises*

> *At its best, the sensation of writing is that of any unmerited grace. It is handed to you, but only if you look for it. You search, you break your heart, your back, your brain, and then — and only then — it is handed to you.*
>
> — Annie Dillard

## Fresh Images and How to Find Them

Images create pictures for readers. Using sensuous details and descriptive adjectives, the writer leads the reader to the place where imagination takes over and the setting, place, and people — all the sights, sounds, smells, and textures of the piece — are conjured in the reader's mind. The more distinct the image, the more the reader feels present and a part of the story. Your job as a writer is to find fresh images. Or make fresh from stale. Take these suggestions for finding images literally or figuratively.

■ stand in one place and look up, look down, turn around 360 degrees, looking as you turn

■ change your perspective: stand up, sit down, squat, lie down

■ be a camera: go long shot, medium shot, close-up, extreme close-up

■ focus/lose focus (make soft eyes, don't look directly at an object), change your depth of field

■ glance out of the corner of your eye

■ squint

■ close your eyes, blindfold yourself, and explore your environs; have a friend take you outside or drive you to another location

■ look in the dark

■ look in the shadows

■ imagine you're seeing, hearing, touching, tasting, smelling something for the first time

■ feel objects without looking at them

*The primary purpose of imagery is not to entertain but to awaken in the reader his or her own sense of wonder.*

— Tom Robbins

- rather than just fingers, feel with other body parts, elbows, cheeks, heels, thighs, wrists
- plug your ears and view a soundless world
- follow the contours; notice the intersections, the confluences
- look beneath, behind, under, and over
- change locations, locate the image in another setting
- water it down, rough it up, polish it, paint it another color
- study a common object and make a list of what it looks like

"I choose not to dissect why certain images appear when I'm writing. I just let them lead and take me where they will. And then I proceed to craft the language around it the best I know how," said novelist Gloria Naylor. ❧

*See Pay Attention, Write from the Senses, Hunting and Gathering*

*If you're going to be a writer, you first of all have to develop unusual powers of observation.*

— Nadine
   Gordimer

## Special Occasions

It's our nature as human beings to create ceremonies to mark special occasions. Whether we call them traditions, rites, rituals, observances, customs, or just "the way we do things," we perform acts in certain ways to honor an occasion or give a sense of occasion to an event.

We light candles on a birthday cake and sing "Happy Birthday," count down the seconds until the New Year, toast the bride and groom with champagne; every special occasion has its ceremonies. Even within our own families and groups, we honor rituals that mean nothing outside our circle. The plastic frog that somehow shows up in family pictures at every reunion. The picnic of fresh strawberries and shortcake every anniversary of meeting your partner.

Creating a ceremony and marking a special occasion with a writing session is a way for writers to express their feelings and reflections or memorialize the event in word pictures.

Light a candle and celebrate your birthday with a special writing session. Build a blazing solstice fire and record the midsummer night, or mark the winter solstice, sunset to sunrise by writing your way through the longest night. Gather flowers and surround yourself with sweet-smelling bouquets and honor the first day of spring by writing in your notebook, then pressing a flower between its pages.

Every occasion can be made into ceremony if you give mindfulness to what the event means to you and what its larger meanings are. Your anniversary; a child's birth; the seasons, festivals, or celebrations of your faith; life passages; deaths.

| April 27 | "I can never say quite as much as I know." (after Robert Olen Butler) |
| April 28 | Write about a time you wanted to leave, but couldn't. |
| April 29 | Write about secrets revealed. |
| April 30 | Write about an injury. |

The elements of ceremony include time set aside with a specific beginning and ending and a place that complements the event. Add elements such as music, candles, flowers or plants, special photographs, pictures or illustrations, significant tokens or symbols, or the wearing of special clothes or colors. Readings of poems or prayers or simply something you love may be included in the observance, too.

Ceremonies don't have to be complex or lengthy. Bring to the occasion that which is meaningful to you. And bring your notebook. When you are ready to write, simply begin with the time and place. "Summer Solstice, 2000. The Cove at La Jolla as the sun sets." Then, as with other writing sessions, simply follow your pen, one word and the next and the next.

Topics for special occasion writing:

- Write remembrances of the occasion in times past.
- Write the significance of the event at this particular time.
- Write of the elements of the ceremony, describing and chronicling.
- Write a compilation since the last occasion (especially if you're writing your birthday or the New Year).

*To honor our dreams and to honor our loved ones and to honor our rituals and our lives is precisely what literature is endlessly trying to teach us.*

— Allan Gurganus

# May

"To be a good writer, you not only have to write a great deal, but you have to care."

—Anne Lamott

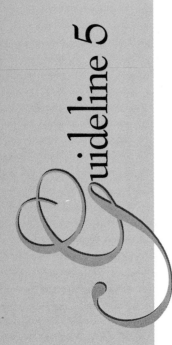

## Don't Worry about the Rules

It doesn't matter if your grammar is incorrect, your spelling wrong, your syntax garbled, or your punctuation off. Not during practice sessions anyhow. Worrying about these rules during writing practice can trip up the intuitive flow of words and images. Pondering comma versus semicolon or whether *i* goes before *e* means you've crossed over that horizon from right brain to left brain to the place where there be dragons — the editor, judge, critic, and censor.

During practice sessions, if you can't spell a word, write it out as best you can; can't think of the name of a street or river or restaurant, draw a blank line that you fill in later. Find a shorthand that works for you, so long as you just keep moving forward, one word after the other. You can always go back, clean up, and correct if you want to use the practice piece in something else you're writing.

Having said all that, here's a word or two about the importance of correct spelling, grammar, and punctuation: Just as saws, hammers, screwdrivers, and awls are tools a carpenter needs, the basics of language usage are the tools of a writer's trade. As a writer, you should know how to use the language and be at ease with its rules. If your foundation is weak, shore it up. Get a good dictionary first of all, and books on basic English structure and usage. I like the classic *Elements of Style*, by William Strunk Jr. and E. B. White, also *The Chicago Manual of Style*, and a grammar book that's more fun than they ever let us know in school, *The Deluxe Transitive Vampire*, by Karen Elizabeth Gordon. Consider taking a course or getting a tutor. One more word of caution: You can only trust the spelling checker on your computer so far.

## Slow Down

Sometimes we're so anxious to get to the end of what we're writing that we go too fast, skipping over parts that cry out for closer inspection or that offer up a truth so simple we hardly recognize it.

It isn't only in writing that we go too fast, but in life as well. Maybe you think you have too much to do (which you probably have), so you feel an urgency to move through your list (and your life) as quickly as possible. You race out the door and down the steps without taking time to notice a fine curlicue of vine growing up the porch rail, a couple of dogs chasing what could be a squirrel or merely a shadow.

The same is true with your writing; there are so many points to make, characters to get from here to there, you zing from one to the next, a pebble across water, without taking the time to delve, to meander, to stay a while.

*Look for a long time at what pleases you, and longer still at what pains you.*
— Colette

Before you begin writing, settle into your chair, feel the face of your page before you, the contours of your pen between your fingers. Breathe in and out a few times. Take your time and go slowly. Not so slow you're sluggish and so is your writing; but slow as in peaceful, unhurried, at ease. When the pace of your writing picks up, follow it and keep its rhythm, but don't turn every corner, willy-nilly; don't cross the street until you've looked both ways.

When a door wants to be opened, open it, go inside, explore the room, sit on the sofa, plump the pillows, pull books from the bookshelf, and page through them. Sniff the air and make note of the scents. If you feel uncomfortable in the room, all the more reason to stay and look around. It's often when the writing gets uncomfortable that we want to hurry along. Don't. Loosen the grip on your pen, stay in the room, and breathe.

### Writing Topics

| | |
|---|---|
| May 1 | Write about circling the edge. |
| May 2 | Write about falling. |
| May 3 | Write about a sin. |
| May 4 | "Why not? ... " |

TIP
OF THE
MONTH

*Find a subject you care about and which you in your heart feel others should care about. It is this genuine caring, not your games with language, which will be the most compelling and seductive element in your style.*

— Kurt Vonnegut

## Top Ten Excuses Not to Practice …

Culled from a bevy of writing-practice experts, these are the top ten excuses not to practice.

1. Cleaning, laundry, shopping, lawn to mow; too busy, too many chores.
2. Not enough time. "Can't write my novel tonight, so why start?" "I'll just get started then it'll be time to quit, so why even start?"
3. Others (spouse, children, family, pets) need me.
4. I'm too tired.
5. I'm not inspired now, but I will be later. I can't focus, don't feel creative, have to get in the mood.
6. Need to exercise.
7. Nap time, bed time.
8. My characters aren't talking to me. I'm stuck on plot, need more research, need to make more notes.
9. I have nothing good to write, nothing to say. I cannot write.
10. I'd rather read (it will inspire me) or watch TV or play on the Internet.

And, of course, the moon is full, there is no moon, Mercury is in retrograde, the Cubs lost, I'm having my period, we're out of coffee.

## ... And What to Do about Them

Excuses not to write are just that. Excuses. Here's how to overcome them:

■ Make a date with yourself for a practice session, set aside that time in your daily schedule, write it in your calendar (in ink), and honor it.

■ If you miss the session, write in your calendar the reason you didn't show up. List what you did instead.

■ Make a date with a writing friend.

■ Start a writing-practice group — with regular attendance as a prerequisite for membership.

■ Reward yourself for practice time put in. (You'll soon find the rewards are inherent in the doing.)

■ If you succumbed to an excuse today, own up to the fact that you're using excuses to not write (what's that all about?), then start again tomorrow by making an appointment with your writing self.

■ Write a letter to yourself expressing why taking the time for writing practice is important, and write as if you were talking to your very best friend. Say how you see yourself as a writer and what writing means to you. Just for fun, self-address and stamp the letter and give it to a friend to mail to you sometime in the future without telling you when to expect it.

*See Daily Routine, The Discipline of Writing*

*It's important to try to write when you are in the wrong mood or the weather is wrong. Even if you don't succeed you'll be developing a muscle that may do it later on.*
— John Ashbery

| | |
|---|---|
| May 5 | Wearing that ring ... |
| May 6 | I can imagine. |
| May 7 | "Some things you'll never forget." |
| May 8 | Write about a cold snap. |

# Try Out Ideas

No place is safer for trying out ideas — even the most radical — than your writing-practice notebook. You've got time and all the pages you need. You've even got permission to write badly and to stop any place you want. So go ahead, take that hub of an idea out for a spin. See what happens.

■ Want to try dialogue like a couple of characters out of an Elmore Leonard novel? Go ahead. Make it as banal, as over-the-top as you want. Let carrots talk to peas, motorcycles talk to cars, photographs talk to subjects.

■ Never tried your hand at genre writing? Create a fantasy, a western, a sci-fi. Even the bodice-ripping, heavy-breathing purple prose of a romance. Who's to read this stuff unless you invite them?

■ Write erotica. Not that bodice-ripping, heavy-breathing purple prose, but the real stuff. The Anne Rice as Anne Rampling, the Susie Bright, the *Yellow Silk* or *Black Lace* of erotica.

■ Have an idea and don't know whether it fits fiction, play, or screenplay? Try some of each.

■ Never wrote a screenplay? Go for it, a few pages worth, in your notebook. On a Saturday afternoon. Look through the camera of your mind.

■ Change point of view; write the story from one character's point of view, then try another. Go from first person to third. Past to present tense.

■ If you're stuck at a juncture of a story and don't know which road to take, travel a little ways down all of them; notice the scenery, the weather, the possible destination.

■ Ask the perennial question of fiction writers everywhere, "What if …?" Ask it even if you're not writing fiction.

Writers aren't born knowing the craft; writers are born with an urge to write, a curiosity, an imagination, and, perhaps, a love of the language. The way to learn the craft is through practice, and your notebook is the place of your apprenticeship. Even writers who are expert in the craft (those who've practiced long and hard) still try out ideas.

*See When Your Writing Bores Even You, Gifts from the Muse, Hunting and Gathering*

## How to Tell When the Critic Is Present …
## and What to Do about It

Here's a list of telltale signs that indicate the critic is, if not sitting on your shoulder, at least in the room somewhere.

■ You stop writing in the middle of a piece and say something like, "This is not working" or worse, "This is crap" or "This sucks."

■ You hear voices demanding: "Who do you think you are?" or "You call that writing?" or "You think anybody will ever buy that? Fool." Thin tinfoil voices that sound as if they're passing through pinched lips and tight mouths.

■ You can't write what you want to write, your writing dead-ends or trails off into drivel.

■ Your pen is afraid to touch the paper and keeps pulling back.

■ You stop writing on the topic and instead write unkind notes to yourself: "This is junk" or "Blah, blah, blah" or other, more critical comments.

■ You start to judge even your handwriting, saying how bad it is, how sloppy; no one could possibly read it.

■ You judge your hands, how scruffy and unkempt your nails are, how the pen you've chosen is all wrong.

■ You channel people who've criticized your writing, or images of them appear on your page; they're usually smirking. A whole gallery of smirking faces, or that one single idiot with a pea-sized brain and bad breath who told you to consider your day job as a career path.

■ You imagine people laughing behind your back, not just agents or editors but your close friends, who all agree your writing is so bad it's hilarious.

*One of the more difficult parts of writing is making the transition from an idea … to a story, which must pass before the eyes of the internal literary inspector. …*

— Ethan Canin

| | |
|---|---|
| May 9 | Write about a premonition. |
| May 10 | "It's all you could expect." |
| May 11 | Write about a time you gave someone a present. |
| May 12 | I can't remember. |

This nasty con artist of a voice is your own self-doubt and negativity that must be silenced if you are to get any work done.

You can trash the critic, draw pictures of its ugly face, then tear them into tiny pieces and toss them in the garbage. Or set them ablaze.

You can write all the lines that voice feeds you on strips of paper and put them in a jar. Close the jar tightly so no air can get in and stash it on a shelf deep in your pantry where the light can't reach it. Or in the back of your closet beneath all those old shoes. Maybe in the furthest reaches of the garage. Or the basement. Leave it to the roaches and spiders.

*You do your best work when you're not conscious of yourself.*

— Peter
  Matthiessen

You can make a deal with the critic. Ask it to wait outside until you've finished your work, then you'll give it voice (which is a lie, but who's to know).

You can scare the little bully off by outbullying it: "Get out of here you twerp!"

You can ignore it, give it the old silent treatment until it finally gets bored and skulks away. (Note: This can take more time than you have.)

You can recognize it for what it is, self-doubt and fear; acknowledge it; then get on with your writing. If you keep writing no matter what, you can bypass this dead-end road and keep heading west, into the sunset. &

## Turn the Soil

Think of a garden and the rich, loamy earth that's exposed when you heave to with hoe and spade.

This is what happens when you practice. When you write about that summer day when the sun was heavy in the sky and you and your father were fishing on the banks of the Platte River, his red-and-white plastic bobber bouncing on the milk chocolate water — you are turning the soil of memory with your spade of a pen. Breathe in and smell its fecund possibilities, get down on your hands and knees for a close-up of the living things you've unearthed.

You keep writing, turning the soil, going deeper, mixing it up. Surprised, maybe at what you've excavated and curious — why this image, this day?

One day's session may take you into a memory of rafting down the Colorado River through the vast split of the Grand Canyon. You try to go back to it the next day, but instead find yourself describing the lopsided grin of the waitress who served you hash and eggs at breakfast that morning. Not until two weeks later do you write about the canyon again; you and your husband stretched out next to each other in your sleeping bags, watching the moon volley the tall walls above you. You keep writing and you unearth more — the icy clamp of the water when you tried to rinse shampoo from your hair; him fishing at the edge of the river, whistling as he always did when he fished. But next day's practice, it's something else — the smell of wild lilac on the hillside that leads you into your grandmother's bedroom. Like Brigadoon, the Grand Canyon is lost to you again.

Like sprouts breaking through the earth, you can't demand an image to

*Much of my writing is energized by unresolved memories — something like ghosts in the psychological sense.*

*— Joyce Carol Oates*

| | |
|---|---|
| May 13 | "Even after my death … " (after Maria Luisa Spaziani) |
| May 14 | Write about abandoned houses. |
| May 15 | Write about a reflection. |
| May 16 | Ten years ago … |

appear. Instead, you hoe, you shovel, you take off your shirt and bend to your weeding. Then, one day, you're writing about a street you once lived on and, without willing, the memory of that last trip to the Grand Canyon comes. This time the images come full tilt: the echo inside the wide mouth of a rock cave when he said your name, the auburn glint of his hair as he shaded the sun from your face and made promises he wouldn't be able to keep of returning to this place. The words you write are true and you are able, this time, to write into the memory through your pain and your tears.

Think of each practice session as an exercise in gardening. After only one or two weeks of writing, you won't have rows of corn, all silk tasseled and ripe for harvest. You may have a single row of soil half-turned, where later you'll drop seeds, one by one, and maybe, if the weather holds and the alchemy is right, within a few more weeks tiny green seedlings might break through. Not all your seeds will sprout, however, and the harvest won't come this month, or even the next. It takes time to grow a garden; it takes time to write what wants to be written. Rainer Maria Rilke reminded us to "… always wish that you may find patience enough in yourself to endure, and simplicity enough to believe." ❧

*Writing is always a voyage of discovery.*

—Nadine
   Gordimer

## When They Became Writers

**M. F. K. Fisher** said she became a writer when she was four. It was her way of screaming and yelling, the primal scream.

**Madeleine L'Engle** knew she was going to be a writer from the moment she wrote her first story. "I was five and it was called 'G-R-U-L.' I didn't know how to spell girl. My father got a new typewriter when I was ten and gave me his old one. I immediately wrote my first novel."

**James Michener** didn't start writing until he was forty. Stationed on an island from 1944 through 1946, he wrote *Tales of the South Pacific*, the first writing he had done. After he completed it, he decided to become a writer.

**Anne Lamott** said, "All of a sudden [during the writing of *Hard Laughter*] there was some structure and there was some order and there was a point A where the book begins and a point B where the book ends. I became a writer."

**May Sarton** was "reborn" as a writer at age twenty-six after a failure in the theater.

**Jay McInerney** claimed writing was something he wanted to do since he could remember, aside from a brief notion of being a trapper in the Hudson Bay, or a mercenary.

**Agatha Christie**, previously a poet and writer of children's books, began writing detective mysteries at age thirty after being challenged by her sister who said she could not handle the rules governing that genre. She wrote thirty Poirot books.

**Amy Tan** decided to do something for herself when her friends called her a

The Writing Life

| | |
|---|---|
| May 17 | You're in a hotel lobby. |
| May 18 | Write about a place you know, but not well. |
| May 19 | One day, … |
| May 20 | Write about ebb tide. |

workaholic. "I at first went to a psychiatrist about this, but after he fell asleep three times during sessions, I decided I would try my own kind of therapy, so I studied jazz piano and tried to write something that I really wanted to write."

**Marge Piercy** said she became a writer at fifteen, when her parents moved into a house where she had a room of her own and a door that shut.

**Eugène Ionesco** claimed he was always a writer. "I wanted to write my memoirs at ten."

**Alice McDermott's** sophomore college writing professor called her into his office and said, "I've got bad news for you. You're a writer and you're never going to shake it."

**Raymond Carver** was in college, too, an undergraduate at Humboldt State. "One day I had a short story taken at one magazine and a poem taken at another. It was a terrific day! Maybe one of the best days ever."

When she was seven, **Dorothy West** asked her mother if she could close her door. Her mother said yes and asked why. "Because I want to think." When Dorothy was eleven, she asked her mother if she could lock her door. Her mother said yes and asked why. She said, "Because I want to write."

**Joseph Wambaugh** first became aware of himself as a writer with the completion of his third book.

**Lynn Sharon Schwartz** said, "It's impossible to be a 'good girl' and a writer at the same time. When I was about thirty-two, it dawned on me I had to make a choice: 'be good' or be a writer. And I decided to be a writer." ❧

*An incurable itch for scribbling takes possession of many and grows inveterate in their insane hearts.*

— Juvenal

# Take a Long, Literary Breath

Los Angeles novelist Janet Fitch has her students take a long, literary breath — that is, write on a topic for ten or twelve minutes in one single, long sentence, using commas, semicolons, dashes, parenthetical phrases, clauses, and connectors such as *then, anyway, besides, also,* and, *but*; anything but a period. These long, meandering paragraphs often uncover delicious little morsels tucked inside someone's pocket that the writer might never have come to in another way. Here's an example of a long, literary breath of a sentence written by writer Dian Greenwood during a workshop.

*You have to give yourself the space to write a lot without a destination.*

— Natalie Goldberg

The day I met her was a day that crowded the sun, that closed down on the forest surrounding the town except for that one side reaching its flat surface and dull sand to the sea, a day like so many in December when the darkness squeezes the light into the middle and there's little relief from a multitude of grays converging just like she did, her hat the color of smoke, her eyes a pearl gray that reminded me of my dead mother's pearls in the bottom drawer of my Tibetan box, her hands limp at her side as we sat in the café, crowded with tourists buying sea shells and come in hope of a *tsunami*, her purse on the counter, a string bag filled with what appeared to be a book, an apple and a pair of orange-handled scissors like someone who looks for open yellow roses on their market walk and surreptitiously clips them for the bud vase waiting on the crocheted dresser scarf in her solitary bedroom, her bag crowding the man beside her at the counter where he clutched his paper in annoyance and she stared ahead, her tea now cold, the milk a

| May 21 | It's too soon to tell. |
| May 22 | Write about predictability. |
| May 23 | Road maps. |
| May 24 | Write about something you see every day. |

cloud in her cup and the muteness, the vacancy in her eyes telling a story about unmentionable deceptions and betrayals I didn't want to know, her pale eyelashes another mask of her invisibility and the muteness a barrier to any impulse on my part to reach out and proffer the first word, even in passing, even… out of kindness for what is disturbed and then lost in the gray world of changing tides, of winter seas engulfing the beach, in the monoliths that rise above the ocean like inverted anchors to hold onto when one is gathering perspective.

*I'm exaggerating so you'll get to know me faster.*

— Amy Hempel

Try this exercise yourself, beginning with any of the topics in the book (the one for today's date, for example) or simply begin by writing your morning. ❧
*See Go Deeper, Doors and Windows*

## Avoiding the Truth

One way or another, writing brings us to our truth, which is not always the destination for which we bought a ticket. The truth can feel dangerous — like you're exposing yourself or telling secrets. Sometimes, without even knowing it, we avoid, sidestep, bypass, or otherwise circumnavigate the truth in our writing. Here are some checkpoints to look for in your writing that indicate you might be avoiding the truth:

- Changing the subject.
- Nattering on and on about meaningless details.
- Closing up.
- Becoming glib.
- Being nice.
- Using generalities instead of specifics.
- Hurrying along.
- Looking the other way.
- Ignoring the naked emperor riding by and the elephant in the living room.
- Glossing over the top, like a coat of wax.
- Affecting attitude; posing.
- Tap-dancing around the topic.
- Killing the messenger (getting rid of a character, one way or another).
- Filling the stage (bringing in a host of characters to distract, like company).
- Leaving the scene (someone exits).
- Bringing in *outside forces* (suddenly, the phone rang; someone knocked; lightning struck).

*If you don't tell the truth about yourself, you cannot tell it about other people.*

— Virginia Woolf

| | |
|---|---|
| May 25 | You're listening to the radio. |
| May 26 | "And it was at that age ... " (after Pablo Neruda) |
| May 27 | It's snowing. |
| May 28 | Write about a time someone said yes. |

- Abandoning the piece.
- Starting something entirely new, on a different topic.
- Not writing.

These avoidances in writing are just like avoidances in real life, except perhaps more obvious and lasting because they're in black and white. Writing the truth is always a challenge to the writer. This is what the great American novelist Willa Cather said: "Artistic growth is, more than it is anything else, a refining of the sense of truthfulness. The stupid believe that to be truthful is easy; only the artist, the great artist, knows how difficult it is." ❧

*See Take Risks, How to Tell When the Censor Is Present, Tell Your Secrets*

*Truth is such a rare thing, it is delightful to tell it.*

— Emily Dickinson

## " ... in wandering mazes, lost"

In a line borrowed from John Milton, you're invited to wander, meander, lose your bearings, not in "elevated thought," as the poet wrote, but to lose yourself in place. Not so lost they have to send out the dogs, but lost enough that you are uncertain of exactly where you are or how to find your way home again.

With notebook in hand, wander neighborhoods you're unfamiliar with, a part of town you don't know. Or drive to another community. Better yet, take the train or a bus. Travel a different road, turn this way and that until you're not quite sure where you are and don't recognize the landmarks. Or walk a well-known trail, then veer off in a direction you've not gone before, where you don't know what to expect. In town or out, get off the beaten path and venture into the wilds.

This special writing-practice session suggests that the effects of unfamiliar territory and the tension of not knowing exactly where you are or how to get home can be good for your writing. And your soul. Most likely you'll pay more attention to the details of the place, notice the specifics: the names of streets and shops, the architecture and geography, flora and fauna. Being lost, your senses will be on the alert; you may have your psychic guard up, too, and feel somewhat wary of strangers. You're in foreign territory and they're the natives.

Allow a generous amount of time for this special session. Who knows how long it might take to find your way home again. You may discover one place that invites a writing, then, after you've completed a session and continue on your way, another location will call out to you and you'll just have to write again. Give yourself over to the adventure. Make generous notes in your notebook about the feelings and sensations of being lost.

| | |
|---|---|
| May 29 | Before I was born. |
| May 30 | If I could do it over again. |
| May 31 | You hear a siren. |

This is another Beyond Practice session that's better done alone. Taking a pal along removes some of the tension from that delicious scary feeling of being lost and creates a safety and distraction that is at odds with the intention of the exercise.

Take maps if you must, change for phone calls, your notebook of course. If you do venture into the wilds, prepare yourself with provisions. This exercise isn't suggesting you put yourself in any real danger. Just create some suspense, heighten your awarenesses, titillate your senses.

Here are some topics for the adventure, or create your own from the environment and your sensations, both inner and outer.

*Teach yourself to work in uncertainty.*

— Bernard Malamud

- Write about a time of small despair.
- Write about being on the outside.
- "Death changes everything." (after Dorothy Allison)
- Write about a spiderweb.
- "My real name is …"

# JUNE

"Only those that risk going too far
can possibly find out how
far one can go."

—T. S. Eliot

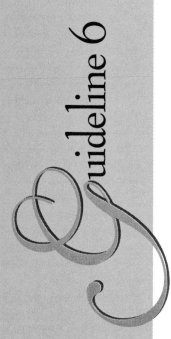

Guideline 6

## Let Go of Expectations

Expectations set you up so you're always ahead of yourself rather than being present in the moment. This is why it's good to dive right into the writing topic with no time to think of what you'll write or how best to shape your writing around the subject.

For example, let's say something important has happened in your life and you believe you should write about it. You give a cursory look at the day's topic, then try to bend it around what you want to write about. Instead of the writing flowing freely, you can't get a word out, or if you do, it's a puny, shriveled little word, inadequate for the important subject you tried to write about.

Another example: You're feeling lethargic, low energy, and definitely not creative. But you've committed to a practice session and, good for you, you're going to show up at the page, no matter what. You arrive grudgingly and a little resentful, muttering under your breath, "Okay, I'll go but I won't write anything good." And, of course, you don't. In this case, unfortunately your expectations have been fulfilled.

How do you let go of expectations? Before you begin writing, take a few moments to clear your mind. Settle into your place and breathe in and out deeply a few times. Let your mind be open and peaceful before you begin and let your writing surprise you. One of the comments most often repeated at writing-practice groups is "I don't know where that came from." It's usually said with some amazement.

## How Can I Tell If My Writing Is Improving?

A promise inherent in the concept of writing practice, or for that fact, the steady practice of anything — glassblowing, layups, a foreign language, hanging wallpaper — is that the more you practice, the better you'll get. Unfortunately, we're not always the best judge of our own work; sometimes we're too close to notice any improvements. Or the critic's voice is louder than any of the rest of the company, so we always hear what's wrong with our writing, not what's good or what's getting better.

You may recognize that your writing is becoming freer, more facile. You may find yourself liking more of what you've written and perhaps you do sense a general improvement. However, if you want something more specific, the following is a checklist you can use to measure your writing progress.

■ You easily fall into writing about the topic and begin writing without hesitation; you don't stop to think or consider, you just keep the pen moving.
■ You stay with the topic long enough to explore it, rather than verging off into digressions that go nowhere or jumping from one thought to the next. You are a more patient writer.
■ You stay out of journal-writing and in creative writing mode; you keep yourself out of the way.
■ Your verbs are lively and diverse.
■ Your images are fresh.
■ You write with fewer clichéd words and images.
■ Your sentences vary in length and structure.

*A writer needs three things: experience, observation, and imagination, any two of which, at times, any one of which, can supply the lack of the others.*

— William
Faulkner

### Writing Topics

| June 1 | Write about something to hold on to. |
| June 2 | Write about a silence. |
| June 3 | Once, when I was … |
| June 4 | What are you looking for? |

### TIP OF THE MONTH

*Don't just put in your time. That is not enough. You have to make a great effort. Be willing to put your whole life on the line when you sit down for writing-practice.*

— Natalie Goldberg

■ Instead of putting a period at the end of a sentence, you put a comma and take the thought further.

■ You write more naturally, with less self-consciousness.

■ Adverbs have all but disappeared from your writing.

■ Your writing is truthful and honest. You don't hold back.

■ Ah, those details you have chosen. Delicious.

■ You layer your writing with sensory images. You include smells, sounds, and textures as well as visuals. You let sensory images do double duty for you, tasting emotions, hearing colors, coloring sounds.

■ You don't overwrite, nor are you stingy with words.

■ You have expanded your language, learned new words.

■ You write in the active voice.

■ You save the strongest word for the last in the sentence.

■ You don't rush through to get to the end, but take your time, lingering and savoring. Letting the tension build.

■ You take more risks.

■ You don't pull your punches.

■ You've eliminated generalities; you write in specifics.

■ You're willing to experiment, to try out, to go to unknown places in your writing.

As for that idea that "practice makes perfect," it's a lie. There is no perfect, only better and sometimes, very, very good. ❧

## Revising

There's a reason they call them drafts and give them numbers like first, second, third, and so on, sometimes up into the thirties or forties before they are pronounced *final drafts*. This reason is revision and some say it's the best part of writing, like Brooklyn-born writer Bernard Malamud, who called revising "one of the exquisite pleasures of writing."

Writing is a two-step process. First, getting down the raw, uncut first draft, which has a right to be messy, unordered, disconnected, and rambling. After all, the writer is following the path beaten out by intuition, and intuition sets a lively pace that doesn't allow for stopping to get your bearings.

The second step is revising. This is where the writer cuts and hacks away, reordering and rearranging, rewriting to discover more of what the piece wants to be. This revising will send you back to the first draft again as you find doors to go through and holes to fill, and you'll continue the process of writing, rewriting, writing, rewriting. For most writers, the second step is the longest. "I tacitly assume that the first fifty ways I try it are going to be wrong," said poet and novelist James Dickey. A few cautionary thoughts:

Too much rewriting can tame the wildness right out of your work, leaving a piece of writing that's as flat as the path you've beaten down to get there.

No matter how massive your memory, computers are only as reliable as your last save command. Make a copy of every draft. You may like an idea you had in the second draft better than what you wrote in the seventh.

Revising before you've reached the end of the first draft may keep you from ever finishing a piece. As novelist Pearl Buck put it, "You're likely to begin dawdling with the revisions and putting off the difficult task of writing."

*The completion of any work automatically necessitates its revisioning.*

— Joyce Carol Oates

| June 5 | Write about small regrets. |
| June 6 | You are standing on one side of a closed door. |
| June 7 | Write about something that came in a box. |
| June 8 | This is the voice of my body. |

## Saying No to the Muse

Let's say you're in the midst of a writing session, chugging along at a good rate, maybe you're arm wrestling it some, trying to get where you know you want to go. Suddenly you feel a buzzing little whisper that tickles your ear or a slight tugging at your psychic sleeve. Instead of tuning in for a minute to see what might want your attention, you brush it off; you keep trudging forward, certain that the direction you're going in is the only road home.

Or let's say you do take notice of that quick flash of thought or niggling little idea, but with hardly more than a sideways glance, you dismiss it like royalty with a serving girl. Whether you say the following words aloud or not, when thoughts like these cross your mind, you're saying no to the Muse.

*When you're working you're not censoring things. You're just hoping all the gates will be open and you'll get something out of your past that will be useful.*

— Charles Johnson

- My character wouldn't do that.
- That's stupid!
- I can't possibly write *that*.
- How does that fit in with what I'm writing?
- I need more time to think about that.
- You're getting in the way of what I'm doing here.
- I don't have the energy right now to follow you.
- You're scaring me.
- I don't understand what you want me to write.
- Just let me do this first.
- Hold that thought, can you.
- That's not logical.
- That's boring. No one is interested in that.
- That could never happen.
- Ah, that feels a little too painful. Maybe later.
- Help me with what I'm doing here, and we'll get back to your idea.
- That's cute, but it wouldn't work here.
- Too far out. Nobody would believe it.
- Can you come back tomorrow?

Though she has the patience of a saint, the Muse doesn't like to be ignored. If you don't pay attention, she may stop paying calls.

## Saying Yes to the Muse

The Muse doesn't keep a time schedule. She may ignore your requests for her presence and then show up when you least expect her and when it's most inconvenient. She does not honor demands. Rather, she likes to be coaxed, prepared for, made welcome. And then, some wondrous, surprising times, she simply appears. Like a gift, or grace.

As a writer or any artist, it's important to always welcome her, to accept her favors and presence. If you shun her, she's likely to find you an unreliable host and withhold her visits. Say yes to the Muse by:

■ Keeping pen and paper always nearby to write down those lines and ideas and thoughts — in your car, beside your bed, carried with you as you go for walks, work in the garden, do the dishes.

■ Honoring the gift by writing it down as it comes; get out of the shower, pull off to the side of the road, excuse yourself from a conversation. Like a dream, you may believe you'll remember, but these visitations are tenuous, gossamer threads of imagination or intuition and disappear like morning mist into sunlight.

■ Leaving an open space in your mind. Try to not always be thinking, planning, evaluating. Breathe in and out and let your mind be at rest, open and welcoming to gentle, unplanned thoughts and ideas.

■ Setting a place for the Muse with lovely things: candles and flowers, music and art, colors, textures, scents; things you love that have meaning for you.

■ Being present at an appointed time. Some say that if you show up at the same place and the same time every day, your creative self will know it's time to go to work. The Muse will know where and when to find you.

*The writer gleans wind scraps; he listens wherever he can. Each day is full of instances; what counts, as with all stimuli, is the sympathetic response.*

— Nicholas Delbanco

| | |
|---|---|
| June 9 | Rising early to begin the journey. |
| June 10 | Write about a compromise. |
| June 11 | Write about mistaken identity. |
| June 12 | "Afterward, I thought about … " |

## The Warp and Woof of Writing Practice

Filling your practice notebook, you'll produce story shoots, the beginnings (or middles) of essays, fragments of memoir or personal narrative, monologues, characters who want you to write them, maybe even a few pages of a play or screenplay. Your notebooks will not only show you what you want to write about, but the genre it wants to take.

*The key to turning out good stuff is rewriting. The key to grinding it out is consistency.*

*— Forrest McDonald*

You can continue to develop these beginnings in two ways: (1) transfer the rough draft to your computer or word processor and work on editing and revising and (2) continue to work in your practice sessions on other sections of the piece, letting the fresh material spill into your notebook.

In time, there comes a rhythm of movement between the spontaneous stuff of writing practice and the thoughtful work of editing, revising, and rewriting. An in-and-out process of creating, then revising — dropping down into the intuitive, unrestrained place of origination, then coming up to the more deliberate setting of choice and measured consideration.

Some writers like to work weeks or even longer on the raw material, even to what feels like the completion of a first draft. Others write in their notebook for a time every day, then by that evening have it transferred to computer to read over and edit. Maybe even beginning the next day with the edits before they move back into their notebook. There's no right or wrong way to do it; each writer has to discover his or her own way. This is another of the freedoms and responsibilities of art. There are many great teachers, but no one can say this is the way you *must* do it; they can only say this is the way I do it.

You will come to know your own rhythms. When you have been traveling the heady path of creation and sense it's time to transfer the piece into a construct of some sort, and when you need to move back again from the cerebral into the less conscious. Trust your rhythms and pace, the weave and texture of your process, the spinning of your tales. So long as you continue to write, you are creating your art.

*See Revising, Use Practice as Building Blocks, Writing Cycles*

## Writers on Dreaming

**William Styron** said the whole concept of *Sophie's Choice* was the result, if not of a dream, of a kind of waking vision.

If **Amy Tan** was stuck on the ending of a story, she took the story with her to bed and let it become part of a dream.

**Robert Stone** said, "The process of creating is related to the process of dreaming although when you are writing you're doing it and when you're dreaming it's doing you."

**Sue Grafton** believes frightening dreams are wonderful. She said they re-create all the physiology that she needs in describing her private-eye heroine Kinsey Millhone in a dangerous situation.

**Jorge Luis Borges**, the great Argentine writer, said that it is written in the kabbalah that when the words in a dream are loud and distinct and seem to come from no particular source, these words are from God.

**Allan Gurganus** reported that his characters have made guest appearances in his dreams.

Both **John Barth** and **James W. Hall** told of dreaming words when they're hot and heavy in the writing process. Hall said when these dreams start to come he tries to wake himself up because they're so boring.

In her collection *Darkness*, **Bharati Mukherjee's** story "Angela" re-created the image from a dream she had of cutting wings off birds and sewing them together so she could fly.

The Writing Life

| | |
|---|---|
| June 13 | These were the doubts I had. |
| June 14 | Write about a dinner party. |
| June 15 | When the dust settles. |
| June 16 | Write about an island. |

**Anne Rice** said, "Sometimes dreams show me that my writing should go deeper. Dreams have not so much changed my work as deepened it."

**Anne Rivers Siddons** believes that every creative impulse that a working writer has comes out of that dark old country where dreams come from. "You can trust your subconscious to supply you with truly horrendous, wonderful dreams if you're in the middle of something that's disturbing you badly," she said.

**Maurice Sendak** said, "Dreams raise the emotional level of what I'm doing at the moment."

**Stephen King** reported he uses dreams the way you'd use mirrors to look at something you couldn't see head-on — the way you use a mirror to look at your hair in the back. ❧

## Truth versus Fact

Sometimes you have to lie to tell the truth, and often you can tell a deeper truth by altering the "how it really happened" facts.

As a writer, you turn life into fiction in order to write the stories you have to tell; otherwise you may be unable to tell the truth. Not necessarily because the truth might be libelous, but more often, because of emotional fears: To tell the truth might hurt someone. To tell the truth is to reveal secrets. What will people think if you tell the truth?

In her book *Bird by Bird*, Anne Lamott wrote of a student whose mother used to punish him by burning him on the stove. "Use it," she told him. "She's old, though," he said. "Her life has not been a happy one."

Lamott's advice was to change the mother, change the family, change where they lived. Change everything except the truth of the experience: that when the little boy was naughty the mother held his hand to the flames.

Make composite characters, alter time frames, change locations, leave events out. Remake your story so you can hone in on the truth of what you have to say.

Remember, too, facts are always colored in the retelling, and even the hue changes with the tellers. Think of the versions of an event and how you alter the telling depending on the audience. How you shade and shadow, texture and highlight the same story as you relate it to your mother, your best friend, your therapist, your lawyer, a stranger on a plane. Consider how their version of the same story differs from yours.

Family stories often have different versions:

"After Grandma Leydon's funeral, Grandpa stopped speaking entirely."

*Tell all the truth but tell it slant.*

— Emily Dickinson

| | |
|---|---|
| June 17 | It's who you met at a party. |
| June 18 | Out of the corner of my eye. |
| June 19 | In the heat of the afternoon. |
| June 20 | Someone's playing the piano. |
| June 21 | Write about a pair of shoes. |

"No, no, Grandpa Leydon stopped speaking long before that. He didn't speak to Grandma Leydon for the entire last year she was alive."

"No, that's not how it was. Grandpa Leydon got cancer and had his larynx removed years after Grandma died. He was fine until then. Talked a blue streak."

So the truth of facts may not be the truth of the story. And the facts may have to be changed in order to be truthful. Remember, your only obligation as a writer is to tell the truth. "A writer's problem does not change," Ernest Hemingway told us. "He himself changes, but his problem remains the same. It is always how to write truly, and having found what is true, to project it in such a way that it becomes a part of the experience of the person who reads it." ❧

*See Transferring Real Life to Fiction, Truth Is in the Details*

*There's no harm in lying a bit.*

— Henry Miller

## Writing Cycles — To Every Thing There Is a Season

Every writer experiences cycles — a productive time, a fallow time. Just like the Bible says, a time to reap and a time to sow. You will be capable of tremendous output and you will be exhausted. Your cycles may run with the course of the moon or be in rhythm with some internal, cellular clock that keeps its own time.

You may notice that sometimes, no matter what, the writing is difficult. Even though you're not stressed, you're present with your writing, you've set aside the time and are looking forward to the session, when you put pen to page nothing happens. Or that which happens is boring. Or junk. The words are clumsy and get in each other's way like the sneakered feet of a thirteen-year-old. You experience a dozen false starts and generally just can't get the thing going. Before you scream "writer's block" and phone your therapist for an appointment, consider that this may just be the fallow side of your cycle.

Other times, your day is short by three hours, you've got umpteen dozen things going on, when you do sit down at the page, you're jittery and not really present. Yet this time, when you begin writing, it flows. Words light upon each other in graceful abandon, your imagery is as rich as crème brûlée with that same crusty, crispy edge. You hardly notice the passage of time; you write non-stop for two hours.

Through writing practice, you'll learn your cycles — when to take advantage of the productive time and when to refill your stores. If you want to actually track your cycles, go back through several months of notebooks and chart the ebb and flow of your writing.

*Being an artist means: not numbering and counting, but ripening like a tree, which doesn't force its sap, and stands confidently in the storms of spring, not afraid that afterwards summer may not come.*

— Rainer Maria
    Rilke

| June 22 | Write about a letter. |
| June 23 | Write about an hour of the day. |
| June 24 | This is what you can see by starlight. |
| June 25 | It was Sunday, the time it happened. |
| June 26 | Write about the making of beds. |

There are a handful of markings that leave an easy trail: Generous, loose handwriting that spreads across the page and large, open lettering, maybe even writing outside the lines vs. small, cramped lettering with many cross-outs, abandoned words, and deserted sentences. Fresh language and vivid images vs. trite words and weary clichés. Page after page of writing in a session vs. a paltry few in the same amount of writing time. As you reread the pieces, you'll see right away when you were on and when you were off.

Of course, no chart will give you complete information about your writing history. There's more to writing cycles than the pull of the moon or the beat of an internal rhythm; even the ocean is influenced by storms. However, if you are unable to write, consider that this may be a time of dormancy, like an orchard in winter: somewhere, underground in the roots and deep within the heartwood of every apple tree, the idea of apples rests, awaiting the time to begin once again the cycle of fruition. Do not judge yourself during this fallow time; accept that it is a time of rest and infuse yourself. Take in, fill up, rejuvenate.

And when you are producing, give all, every time. ❧

*See Writer's Block, What Stuck Looks Like, How to Get Unstuck*

## On the Road

Complete books have been written "on the road" — John Steinbeck's *Travels with Charley*, William Least Heat Moon's *Blue Highways*, and Jack Kerouac's *On the Road*, to name just three. This Beyond Practice session urges you to pack your bags and your notebooks and take to the streets or highways or interstates. Grab a boat, catch a plane, hop a train. And write.

What may happen is that you'll write about the place you've just left. Henrik Ibsen wrote about Norway while in Italy, James Joyce wrote of Dublin from Paris, where Ernest Hemingway wrote of Detroit. The prairie novels of Willa Cather were composed in New York City.

Or maybe you'll be like Steinbeck, Least Heat Moon, and Kerouac, writing about the road you're traveling from your view just above it, notebook open on the seat beside you. Writing yourself to sleep at night and awaking in the morning with your hand already moving, words and impressions abiding in your mind as if they had been captured in the lair of a dream catcher.

Travel sets free the pen. Especially when you go it alone. Traveling solo means talking to strangers. Meeting people, asking questions. Of course you're curious, you're a writer. You take in everything and it's all different — the tilt of the earth, the curve of the horizon, the very color of the sunset. To whom can you say, "Look at that view," when you are alone? You must describe to your notebook the catch of lilac as the sky snags the edge of granite cliff, the turn of hawk balanced on a thermal, its wing afire from the setting sun. When you leave your pals behind, you cannot discuss the details of your job over a meal at the Taverna Totrista. You must taste the *tzatziki*, the resiny flavor of the retsina; you

| | |
|---|---|
| June 27 | This is where I went wrong. |
| June 28 | Write about small change. |
| June 29 | Write about high tide. |
| June 30 | "Long afterward, I came upon it again ... " |
| | (after Colette) |

must pay attention to the sensuous whine of the bouzouki and say aloud *Opa!* and smile at the old man dancing. Later, you'll remember the very resonance of your *Opa* against your rib cage, the scimitar curve of the old man's moustache. This you record in your notebook.

To travel is to see for yourself, to encounter a world outside the accustomed and experience yourself in it. Travel loosens the dust of familiarity and shakes free the folds of the everyday.

You need not take a lengthy trip to experience the effects of travel on your writing. Nor need you go far. A weekend jaunt to the next county or a three-month tour of New Zealand. "I travel not to go anywhere, but to go," said writer-adventurer Robert Louis Stevenson. "I travel for travel's sake. The great affair is to move."

A few topics for the road:

- I can't explain …
- Write about first light.
- Write about the random possibility of miracles.
- "I am in a state of surrender." (after Donald Rawley)
- Midsummer night.
- This is the sound of loneliness.

*Two things make a story. The net and the air that falls through the net.*
— Pablo Neruda

# JULY

"Think of yourself as an incandescent power, illuminated, perhaps, and forever talked to by God and his messengers."

—Brenda Ueland

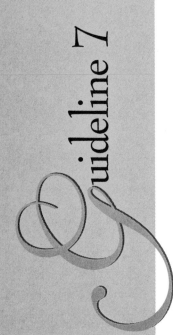

Guideline 7

## Kiss Your Frogs

It happens to every writer: sloppy, rambling, unintelligible, boring writing that is going anywhere but where you want. It's the frog-kissing phenomenon of creative writing and it happens to the best of us, even to seasoned pros. If you write at all, know that you're going to produce some stuff that's way to the left of good, lopsided and croaking on some withering lily pad.

First-draft writing doesn't have to be good, it won't always be good, and even when it is good, among the good will be some not-so-good. For many writers, understanding and accepting this has a powerfully freeing effect. Writing teacher and author Natalie Goldberg says, "You're free to write the worst junk in America." Anne Lamott also has a name for that rough stuff we all write. She calls it "shitty first drafts." It's the swampy, mucky stuff that holds little promise for happily-ever-after, and almost every writer experiences a day when muck is what gets written.

At any given writing session you may write something you like, or your writing may embarrass you in its awful triteness. Sometimes you won't be able to put a coherent sentence together and other times your writing will be fresh, creative, even elegant. The point is, just show up at the page no matter what.

Remember, this is just practice. You write what you write. Besides, who can say from the marshy edge of any pond which frog gets transformed and which kiss holds magic.

## Being Vulnerable on the Page

Writers expose more of themselves than any other artists. When we write about what matters to us, we unveil our deepest feelings. Sometimes even to ourselves and often when we least expect it. When we write about human frailties, we are writing about the fragile scraps of ourselves. Our words tell more than the truth about what we're writing, they also tell the truth about us.

No wonder writing often feels dangerous, makes you lurch from your chair, pace the room, and phone your best friend just to hear a reassuring voice.

"Hi, what are you doing?" (pause) "Me? Oh, nothing. Just writing."

Meantime, the truth of your exposed and bleeding self spreads line by incriminating line across thirteen inches of cold white monitor. And that cursor just keeps blinking, reminding you you're not finished yet. Your notebook lies open on your desk, yammering your secrets to any passerby. You pour a cup of coffee, smoke a cigarette, and snack on anything that will alter the way you feel.

Being vulnerable on the page is one of the risks of the job — it comes with the territory, like performing a high-wire act with a new partner and without a net in a drafty circus tent. And in all likelihood, it's not something that will go away. You may become accustomed to the feeling, but you'll never escape the vulnerability. Novelist and short story writer John Cheever said, "I think that endeavoring to be a serious writer is quite a dangerous career."

What to do? Take a drink of water, breathe deeply, stretch, go ahead and call a friend, then get back to the writing. A little distance may make you feel safer, but the very fact that you are feeling vulnerable means you're writing close to the bone. Stay with it.

*See Take Risks, Tell Your Secrets, Breathe*

*I will go so far as to say that the writer who is not scared is happily unaware of the remote and tantalizing majesty of the medium.*

— John Steinbeck

### Writing Topics

| | |
|---|---|
| July 1 | The possibilities are endless. |
| July 2 | These were the frequently asked questions. |
| July 3 | Write about the inevitable. |
| July 4 | Write about a voice. |

**TIP OF THE MONTH**

*Instead of moving horizontally on the page stay with the one moment or revelation and go down-down-down, vertically, deeper into complication, keep going down and uncovering harder things to say about the same thing.*

— Amy Hempel

## How to Tell When the Writer-Self Is Present

The writer-self is the part of you that is unequivocally for your writing and believes in you absolutely. This is the sweet voice that urges you to put pen to paper and tells you writing is noble and necessary and names the many ways it adds to the quality of life. More than that, it says the work of the writer is "essential for human evolution." Write, it says to you.

You can tell your writer-self is present when:

■ You look forward to your writing time and go on the arm of joy to the special writing place you created.

■ You're not writing — it's before or after your writing time — but anticipatory or lingering thoughts of writing come to you, prologues or epilogues to doing the work.

■ You read other writers and, while you're reading for pleasure or inspiration or to learn, you also notice their execution of the craft.

■ You can't help yourself, if a scribble of paper is there along with a pen, you write something. Words or phrases, an image, or the line of a poem.

■ You're writing, time passes — an hour, two, three; you're hardly aware.

■ You make plans for a holiday or retreat, a weekend getaway. It includes writing.

■ You'd rather be with your writing friends — writing together, talking about writing — than with anyone else doing anything else.

■ You remember people at a writing workshop, not by name, but by something they wrote.

■ You think the most important Oscar is the award for screen writing. Same with the Tonys (playwriting). Even the Nobel Prize for literature ranks above others as far as you're concerned.

■ You hang out at readings, book signings, and author appearances not just to hear the writer read, but to be in the presence of another writer, to make connection with your own kind.

■ Before you drift off to sleep or just when you awaken — first thought, last thought, is about your writing.

■ Your bookshelves sag with books by writers about writing, interviews with writers, how-tos on writing, biographies and memoirs of writers.

■ Among your many, many subscriptions are magazines that feature quality writing, obscure literary journals and small press quarterlies, and trade publications about writers and writing.

■ Your Internet bookmarks run into the dozens — all of them writing sites.

■ You write every day (or as near to that as you can get).

■ Your stamina is amazing. You get up to write at 5:30 every morning or there you are at o'dark hundred, writing beneath the sagging moon. And you still have energy to work your day job.

Your writer-self may not always have priority in your life — there is, after all, falling in love, being with family, honoring the Sacred — but when he or she is present, pay attention. This voice comes from a true part of you. ❧

*I honestly think in order to be a writer, you have to learn to be reverent.*

— Anne Lamott

## Use Practice as Building Blocks

Most all the daily writing-practice topics allow you to continue to develop the raw material of a project you are working on. In fact, using the prompt for that day, you may enter into the piece in a way that would not have been possible had you first thought about what you wanted to write. Writing on the topic is like choosing "door number three." You don't know what's behind the curtain until it's lifted.

Keeping your focus within the confines of your project, let the writing topic be your starting place. If you're writing fiction, write about the topic from the point of view of one of your characters. Change the pronoun from *I* or *you* to *he* or *she*, or use the character's name. For example, if the prompt is "Write about your neighborhood at five o'clock," write about your character's neighborhood in late afternoon. Let the dialogue prompt ("You'll be sorry.") be the character's dialogue. Or something another character says to them. A prompt can even be a question you, as author, pose to your character (Where were you last night?).

If you're writing nonfiction — memoir or personal narrative — and the topic doesn't appear to fit (for example the December 16 prompt: "I walked into the Maverick Bar in Farmington, N.M."), write about a time you walked into any bar, or a time you wanted to walk into a bar, or a time you didn't walk into a bar. Write about a time you were in New Mexico or wanted to be. Turn the whole thing around and begin with "I never walked into the Maverick Bar in Farmington, N.M., but I … " and continue in whatever direction you want to go. Use the prompt as starting blocks from which you push off to begin your laps around the writing-practice track. In rewriting you'll decide whether to lop off references to a bar, the Maverick or any other, or any talk of New Mexico.

Several members of my Brown Bag and Thursday Writers groups have used practice prompts to write portions of their novels or stories. In fact, many scenes in my own novel had their genesis in these groups.

*See Rereading Your Practice Pages, When Characters Appear, Revising*

*There is so much about the process of writing that is mysterious to me, but this one thing I've found to be true: writing begets writing.*

— Dorianne Laux

## Mentors and Heroes

**Chateaubriand** was **Victor Hugo's** inspiration and **Marcel Proust's** hero.

The catalyst for **Edna O'Brien** was a lecture she heard in London on **F. Scott Fitzgerald** and **Ernest Hemingway**.

**May Sarton** was inspired by novelist **Virginia Woolf**.

**Umberto Eco's** *The Name of the Rose* inspired **A. S. Byatt**, who said, " ... one could be at once both very serious and quite funny, and write a detective story in the bargain."

From **Annie Dillard's** book *The Writing Life*, "**Hemingway** studied, as models, the novels of **Knut Hamsun** and **Ivan Turgenev**. **Isaac Bashevis Singer**, as it happened, also chose **Hamsun** and **Turgenev** as models. **Ralph Ellison** studied **Hemingway** and **Gertrude Stein**. **Thoreau** loved **Homer**; **Eudora Welty** loved **Chekhov**. **Faulkner** described his debt to **Sherwood Anderson** and **Joyce**; **E. M. Forster**, his debt to **Jane Austen** and **Proust**."

**Apollinaire** influenced **André Breton**, who influenced **Allen Ginsberg** and **William Carlos Williams**, who was a local underground celebrity who encouraged **Ginsberg's** early writing.

**Truman Capote** was influential in **Joseph Wambaugh's** *The Onion Field*. "My God," he told Wambaugh, "that's a marvelous story. I wish I could write that."

**John Cheever** was the inspiration for **Ethan Canin**, who says, " ... **Cheever's** rhythmic elongation of epiphany in the midst of quiet suburban life brought me over and over again to a sense of longing. At first it was a longing to read. Later it became a longing to write."

| | |
|---|---|
| July 9 | Write what you wanted to do. |
| July 10 | Write about a postcard. |
| July 11 | It was as if ... |
| July 12 | "Throw away the lights, the definitions/and say of what you see in the dark." (after Wallace Stevens) |

Ray Bradbury made up a genealogy, a sort of family tree. "I often think of Robert Frost as my wonderful grandfather and Willa Cather as my grandmother. Eudora Welty is an eccentric cousin of mine and Edgar Rice Burroughs might even be my father. Jules Verne I remember as a marvelous uncle who used to bring me fabulous toys that ran underwater and through the skies and off to the far planets. Somewhere along the line John Steinbeck is my older brother and Ernest Hemingway a still older brother than that. William Faulkner is a very wise old second uncle. A teacher would be Aldous Huxley."

. . . . . . . . . . . . . . . . . . . . . . . . . . . . . . . . . . . . . . . . . . . . . . . . . . . . . . . .

## Honor Yourself as Writer

Putting in time at writing practice is only one of the ways to honor yourself as writer. This list offers several more.

■ Name yourself writer. When people ask what you do, say, "I am a writer." Writing may not be the way you support yourself, but identifying yourself by your day job doesn't give your writing the position it deserves. One person may say, "I'm a writer who supports herself as a paralegal." Another, "I'm a writer. And I earn a living as a masseuse." When you name yourself writer first, you affirm the place writing holds in your life.

■ Make a place for your writing, furnish it with materials that support you and your writing. A good desk or table, a comfortable chair, ample light that is flattering to your writing, shelves or bookcases. Keep the space sacred and go there joyfully.

■ Get the equipment and accoutrements you need — a computer or word processor, a printer you can depend upon. Notebooks, journals, pens, paper you like. A good dictionary, thesaurus, and other reference materials. This is not to imply you must have the latest equipment to really be a writer. Not only can high tech be expensive, it doesn't guarantee your writing will be any better. Remember, Shakespeare had only a quill pen and candlelight.

■ Make time for studying and practicing your craft: attend writing groups, workshops, writers' conferences, classes, and lectures.

■ Schedule time with other writers: get together before or after your group or make time just for hanging out, meet for coffee or a beer, walk a trail together. This is a time for discussing your own writing and writing in general, meander-

*Writing is love, a mission, and a calling, and how and where and why you write are very crucial issues.*

— Lynn Sharon Schwartz

| July 13 | Write about a theft. |
| July 14 | Write about an epiphany. |
| July 15 | It was that kind of day. |
| July 16 | Half an hour before sunrise. |

ing conversations or meaningful dialogue. Either way, this is quality time.

■ Read your writing to others, gifting a poem to someone you know would appreciate it; reading your pieces to family and friends and reading your work at open readings; saying it out loud.

■ Transfer writing from your notebook to the computer and print it out. A piece appears more professional when it's printed; it says "this is a serious piece of writing." File the printed pieces in an orderly way, harboring them in three-ring binders, labeled and berthed on a shelf.

■ Submit material for publication. Intimidating as the whole process can be — the market research, the cover letter, the pristine manuscript, then sealing the envelope and immediately knowing you left out page three; next, releasing the package into the black hole of a mail slot or, maybe worse, handing it over to a glassy-eyed, ponytailed postal employee who tosses it willy-nilly into a dirty, unmarked canvas bag — in spite of all this, you submit your writing for publication because you believe it is good and you believe writing needs an audience to be complete. Submitting your material for publication honors the writing and honors you as writer.

■ Celebrate when you've completed a work or hit a significant marker: a chapter finished, first draft completed, difficult scene written. Some writers celebrate with champagne; others, blended mochas; and still others, a trip to the bookstore. Choose your treat. You deserve it.

■ Accept compliments gracefully. When someone tells you they like your writing or that your words touched them, no need to demure, explain what's wrong, or go into a lengthy discourse about what you really meant to write. Simply say thank you. ❧

## If You Want to Write

### By Brenda Ueland

1. Know that you have talent, are original, and have something important to say.

2. Know that it is good to work. Work with love and think of liking it when you do it. It is easy and interesting. It is a privilege. There is nothing hard about it but your anxious vanity and fear.

3. Write freely, recklessly, in first drafts.

4. Tackle anything you want to — novels, plays, anything. Only remember Blake's admonition: "Better to strangle an infant in its cradle than nurse unacted desires."

5. Don't be afraid of writing bad stories. To discover what is wrong with a story write two new ones and then go back to it.

6. Don't fret or be ashamed of what you have written in the past. How I always suffered from this! How I would regurgitate out of my memory (and still do) some nauseous little lumps of things I had written! But don't do this. Go on to the next. And fight against this tendency, which is much of it due not to splendid modesty, but a lack of self-respect. We are too ready (women especially) not to stand by what we have said or done. Often it is a way of forestalling criticism, saying hurriedly: "I know it is awful!" before anyone else does. Very bad and cowardly. It is so conceited and timid to be ashamed of one's mistakes. Of *course* they are mistakes. Go on to the next.

7. Try to discover your true, honest, untheoretical self.

*I shall live badly if I do not write.*

— Françoise Sagan

| July 17 | In a state of disarray. |
|---------|-------------------------|
| July 18 | Write about a recurring dream. |
| July 19 | Write about a time you got what you wanted. |
| July 20 | Write about passing time. |

8. Don't think of yourself as an intestinal tract and tangle of nerves in the skull, that will not work unless you drink coffee. Think of yourself as incandescent power, illuminated perhaps and forever talked to by God and his messengers. Remember how wonderful you are, what a miracle! Think if Tiffany's made a mosquito, how wonderful we would think it was!

9. If you are never satisfied with what you write, that is a good sign. It means your vision can see so far that it is hard to come up to it. Again I say, the only unfortunate people are the glib ones, immediately satisfied with their work. To them, the ocean is only knee-deep.

10. When discouraged, remember what van Gogh said: "If you hear a voice within you saying: 'You are no painter', then paint by all means, lad, and that voice will be silenced, but only by working."

11. Don't be afraid of yourself when you write. Don't check-rein yourself. If you are afraid of being sentimental, say, for heaven's sake be as sentimental as you can or feel like being! Then you will probably pass through to the other side and slough off sentimentality because you understand it at last and really don't care about it.

12. Don't always be appraising yourself, wondering if you are better or worse than other writers. "I will not Reason & Compare," said Blake; "my business is to Create." Besides, since you are like no other being ever created since the beginning of Time, you are incomparable. ❧

*If thou art a writer, write as if thy time were short, for it is indeed short at the longest.*

— Henry David Thoreau

## Take Risks

Writing means taking risks. If you're not willing to take the risks, chances are your writing will be bland and boring — even to yourself. However, to take such risks requires "the ongoing courage for self-discovery," said much-published writer Harlan Ellison, " … the act of writing with serious intent involves enormous personal risk. It means one will walk forever on the tightrope, with each new step presenting the possibility of learning a truth about oneself that is too terrible to bear."

Of course, we never discover a truth that is too terrible to bear. We only fear we will. Or, that we will expose something of ourselves to others that will be too terrible for them to bear, and we will be judged, perhaps rejected.

Contradictory as it may sound, writing with others is one good way to begin taking risks. There is something about a group setting that engenders bravery — safety in numbers, maybe. Also, listening to the risks others take in their writing can mark a trail to your own cliff edges.

Janet Fitch tells members of her advanced fiction workshop to "stay in the room," meaning don't let your characters or yourself leave the scene before it's complete. In real life when there's danger or conflict the safest action may be to hightail it, but in writing, safety is not a desired ingredient. So even if you have to take a few deep breaths and write paragraphs around what you need to say, "stay in the room" until you've written it.

Take courage, be brave. It's in taking the risks we find our true and honest voice. This is the way to freedom.

*See Avoiding the Truth, How to Tell When the Censor Is Present, Being Vulnerable on the Page*

*If you don't risk anything, you risk even more.*
— Erica Jong

| July 21 | Write about packing a suitcase. |
| July 22 | The first time I saw _____. |
| July 23 | Write about being late. |
| July 24 | Write about a conversation. |

## Gifts from the Muse — Phrases, Images, and Other Kindnesses

You're working in your garden, a buoyant phrase alights upon your shoulder; in the shower, the perfect solution to the story you're writing suddenly comes to you; driving down the freeway, a poem appears, nearly intact.

This is Muse mojo and who knows how it happens.

Perhaps because you've primed the pump with the work you've already done, relaxing in the shower loosens ideas that were caught between the folds of your brain or in the cramp of your muscles.

Maybe the rhythmic step of your foot upon a dusty footpath sets down a beat that cannot be resisted or the comforting ease of lowering dishes into hot soapy water calls forth memories of other kitchens, other times. It seems when you turn to mindless things, you create an incubator for the intuition. "When I was painting the downstairs hall I thought of a novel to write," said writer Anne Tyler.

These images, phrases, and other kindnesses are gifts from the Muse. Her timing is not always impeccable, but her gifts are always delicious, albeit perishable. Grab them while you can. Don't rely on your memory, keep pen and paper nearby.

Writers I know have as many sets of note-taking necessities around the house as it's rumored Frank Sinatra had reading glasses. Notepads and pens in the bedroom on the nightstand (a poet I know jotted iambics on his pillowcase that transferred in the night to his cheek); a waterproof pen and nonabsorbent paper on a shelf just outside the shower curtain; a magic slate dangling magnetically from the refrigerator door; three-by-five cards and felt-tips sealed inside baggies and kept with the gardening tools; goofy-looking notepads affixed to the dashboard of the car; tiny spiral-bound notepads no bigger than your palm stashed in a hip pocket along with a golf-scoring pencil; sticky notes affixed to the most unlikely of surfaces — decorator pillows, dry cleaning bags, dinner plates, makeup mirrors — and, when all else fails, patches of skin exposed beneath shirt cuffs and gym socks.

*See Saying Yes to the Muse*

*All I am is the trick of words writing themselves.*

— Anne Sexton

. . . . . . . . . . . . . . . . . . . . . . . . . . . . . . . . . . . . . . . . . . . . . . . . . .

## Better Verbs

Imagine a language with seventy-five ways to say the word *wind*, each based on the very way the wind moves, its rise and fall, its undulations. The "wind" that shudders the willow boughs, the "wind" that ripples the water, the "wind" that carries rain, the "wind" that rattles windows, and so on. On the other hand, a thesaurus of the English language might list a half dozen words for wind: gust, gale, blast, flurry, blow; plus the directions from which it comes: northeaster, northwester, southeaster, southwester, and so on. For those of us who write in English, lively verbs are one of the ways we can uplift our writing and sail it aloft over rooftops and rivers.

Verbs are the combustible material of the language; they create the action, they move the writing. Verbs contain the energy of sentences.

"Use better verbs!" came back the critique on one of my manuscripts. I reread it, embarrassed to realized how often I used the verb *was*. Once I noticed it, the word stuck out like the proverbial sore thumb. *Was* was everywhere, like a lawn infected with dandelions.

Like *was*, another grouping of three letters that makes for bad verb use is *ing*, the gerund form of the verb that makes it passive. "I was sleeping." "I was going to wake soon." "I was snoring." "I was drooling on my pillow, staining it." Was I dreaming?

Will someone wake these verbs up! Whack off their *ings*, and excite them into action.

"At five in the afternoon, I would be writing." *Would* creates a conditional tense, capturing the verb forever, like a tiny creature in amber, never allowing for change to take place. The state in which I would forever be: writing.

*The most important influence on my writing technically has been ethical — as my brother once said of a florid piece of description, "starve it down and make it run."*

— Marianne
   Moore

| July 25 | Write about asking for mercy. |
| July 26 | A free-for-all. |
| July 27 | You're in a movie theater. |
| July 28 | Every night, … |

But where to find better verbs, she moaned. This is where the crafting of the writing begins. Go ahead and write your practice piece, verbing as you will. Then as you reread, underline all the verbs; notice the words that show some spunk, lift heavy loads, block and tackle, tap-dance, and generally liven up your sentences; these are keepers. Next, notice all those boring, clichéd verbs, the *wases* and the passive forms, the *had hads* and *would bes*. These are the ones you want to change. And you do it verb by verb.

- Use your thesaurus and dictionary.
- Use your imagination.
- Try some exercises such as listing all the verbs that go with a certain activity — cooking for example, or gardening. Sewing. Swimming. Writing.
- List all the jobs you've had and verbalize your activities.
- List all the actions you've taken so far today.
- Read really good writers and pay attention to their verb-crafting.
- Instead of trying to think of better words, close your eyes and picture the image, then come up with words that describe the action. ❧

*See Auditioning Words, Wordplay, About Language, When the Words Aren't Working — A Helping Hand*

*You can be a little ungrammatical if you come from the right part of the country.*

— Robert Frost

## "A Jug of Wine, a Loaf of Bread — a Notebook"

A writer doesn't need much. For Persian poet Omar Khayyám it was "A book of verses underneath the bough," the wine, the bread, and "thou beside me singing in the wilderness," which was for him, enough. With these few effects, wilderness became paradise.

For those who accept the invitation, this Beyond Practice takes writers to a simpler place to find the richness within the moment, to transform the plain into the sublime.

For the morning or afternoon, pack away into your backpack or satchel simple supplies: bread and cheese, some uncomplicated fruit — grapes or cherries, an apple. Bring springwater or wine. Choose a book of verse, Walt Whitman's *Leaves of Grass*, Elizabeth Barrett Browning's *Sonnets from the Portuguese*, Khayyám's *Rubaiyat*, if you please. Or one of your own well-thumbed favorites. Gather your notebook and pens. Let your thou be a soul-connected writing friend.

Take all this and go into the wilderness, a place far enough from the city so the traffic noise cannot reach you, so you don't look upon freeways or streets with stoplights, or any streets at all. No parks with playgrounds where children screech and yammer. No basketball courts or soccer fields. Go beyond all that to a quiet place where, if you hear anything, it will be a chorale of birds, the tumble of stream, the sweet whisper of wind in leaves.

Find a gracious tree that welcomes you beneath its green and spread your simple feast before you. Don't just eat, savor. With all your senses. Read aloud from your book of verses; close your eyes and know this is paradise. Do not be in a rush to begin your writing. Let the verses you have read sink into your bones,

| | |
|---|---|
| July 29 | Write about a scent. |
| July 30 | Write about an eclipse. |
| July 31 | Somebody makes a promise. |

close your eyes and breathe the words. Read again, aloud to your partner; let "thou" read to you. Then, when you are ready, open your notebook and begin writing. Allow a generous, unhurried time, and when you are finished, read aloud to each other again, this time reading what you have written, giving your own writing the same loving attention you gave the masters.

Since you brought the bread and wine, we'll provide the topics.

- These are the things I lost.
- Write about the shadows of afternoon.
- This is what she asked for.
- It was the night of the crocus moon.
- Write about sleeping outside.

# AUGUST

"Anyone can become a writer.
The trick is staying a writer."

—Harlan Ellison

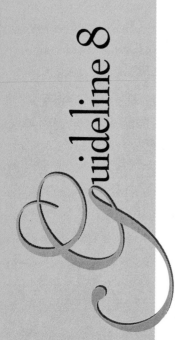

Guideline 8

## Tell the Truth

Every time you write you have an opportunity to tell the truth. Sometimes it's only through writing that you can know the truth, which may be one of the reasons we write in the first place. "The only time I know that something is true is at the moment I discover it in the act of writing," said French novelist Jean Malaquais.

Writing a truth sets up a physical commotion: there's a humming deep in the throat, little hairs on the back of the neck rise and tremble, goose pimples (my grandmother called them "truth bumps") freckle the arms. Breathing changes. This is why it's good to be tuned in to your body while you write. "This is important," it's saying. "Pay attention."

The truth can also be risky. Novelist and short story writer Andre Dubus said, "When I'm writing — that's when I face the exposure, that's when the right word comes, or the temptation to use the wrong word and duck out, the temptation to skip something. That's when I always have to bear down and try to write as closely to what is the truth as I can feel with my senses and with my heart."

Be willing to go to the scary places that cause your hand to tremble and your handwriting to get a little out of control. Be willing to tell your secrets. It's risky, but if you don't write about it, you're chancing writing that is glib, shallow, or bland.

Go to the edge of what feels safe and step off. We always use a net in writing practice.

. . . . . . . . . . . . . . . . . . . . . . . . . . . . . . . . . . . . . . . . . . . . . . . . . . . . . .

## Spiritual Connotations of Writing Practice

"Writers all devise ways to approach that place where they expect to make the contact, where they become the conduit, or where they engage in this mysterious process," said Toni Morrison.

Practice is more than running the scales, shooting the hoops, doing the drills; it has a deeper component. Coming again and again to the same place, mindful and with intention, writing practice becomes in itself a spiritual act. When you enter into your writer's soul, you are treading upon sacred ground.

Consider what you do when you practice writing: You set aside a special time when you will focus all your attention on your practice; you give yourself over to this time. Opening your notebook, you open yourself to possibility, to intuition. Inspiration. You breathe in. *Inspiration* — literally, to take God in. You begin writing and lose yourself to the only time there is: Now. You are wholly with yourself, alive and present in the moment, writing, transcribing what comes from within. When you finish writing and look up from your notebook, there is a sense that you have been elsewhere; it may take a moment to return fully to this world. You feel a certain elation, a completeness.

"Creativity is an experience — to my eye, a spiritual experience. It does not matter which way you think of it: creativity leading to spirituality or spirituality leading to creativity. In fact, I do not make a distinction between the two," said Julia Cameron, creator of *The Artist's Way.*

*See Ten Daily Habits That Make a (Good) Writer*

*Good art is a form of prayer. It's a way to say what is not sayable.*

— Frederich Busch

## Writing Topics

| | |
|---|---|
| August 1 | Write about a tool. |
| August 2 | Write about a time you were misunderstood. |
| August 3 | Write about a bedroom. |
| August 4 | If only, … |

**TIP**
**OF THE**
**MONTH**

*Don't think of literary form. Let it get out as it wants to. Overtell it in the matter of detail — cutting comes later. The form will develop in the telling. Don't make the telling follow the form.*

— John Steinbeck

## What Stuck Looks Like

We've given the term *writer's block* so much power that even talking about it can scare us into one. But stuck, that's another matter. Stuck is a state of being many writers experience. Think of rear wheels in mud, rings on swollen fingers. Stuck is a manageable, fixable annoyance that simply needs something solid beneath it, a little grease maybe.

Here's a list of some of the disguises stuck wears, along with some suggestions for unsticking yourself. (See the accompanying list of How to Get Unstuck for more generalized ideas.)

■ You've written yourself into a corner. Got your characters into a jam and the only way out is too contrived or far-fetched, straining even your own willingness to suspend disbelief.

1. Play "what if ... " and write out all kinds of solutions to the problem. Never mind how contrived or far-fetched they seem; just brainstorm the ideas.
2. Hit the rewind button. Backtrack your story to where the problem started, and take another run at it. (Play "what if ... " at this point.)

■ You're out of ideas for new scenes and don't know where to start the next piece.

1. This is one of the main purposes of the daily writing topics. Do a practice session, free-writing from one of the writing prompts. Use your characters' voices if you're writing fiction.
2. Make a "to do" list for your character, then start writing from one of the items, especially if there's a "to do" listing that involves another character.
3. Send your character out on the streets — to the grocery store, to get a haircut or a pack of cigarettes. Follow him or her, see what happens.

■ You keep rehashing the same stuff, simply restating what you've already written.

1. Try a new genre. If you usually write fiction, try nonfiction, write an essay or a personal narrative piece. If you're a poet, try expanding into fiction or creative nonfiction. Write a play. A screenplay. A monologue or performance piece.

2. If your characters are always the same, try something different. Instead of writing from the point of view of a thirtysomething female, give voice to an old man. Write the opposite of what you usually write: gender, age, geography, physical appearance, politics. Some advise to write what you know; novelist Tom Robbins told workshop participants, "Don't write what you know, write anything you can imagine."

■ You write around what needs to be written, avoiding the real stuff with distractions and diversions.

1. There's a saying in writing groups when someone is tap-dancing around the truth. "Don't leave the room," participants say, meaning stay in the piece even if it's uncomfortable, even if it makes you sweat and squirm in your chair. Stay in the room and write what needs to be written.

2. Write nose-on, blatant stuff and get it all out on paper. Never mind that it's neither graceful nor elegant, just write it. All the hard, stinging, painful, ugly words of it. Write it trite and write it long. Just write it. Now, go back and clean it up, fix it, rewrite it, and polish it. Keep the good, strong, powerful truth; get rid of the sloppy, repetitious, cliché-ridden purple stuff. Give yourself a reward. This is a very courageous act.

■ You can't seem to finish anything. You write a few pages or a few chapters, a stanza or two of a poem, then put the piece away and start something new.

*The main thing is to write a lot, to keep yourself immersed in the element of poetry, to stay deep in the creative possibilities.*

— James Dickey

| | |
|---|---|
| August 5 | Write about a summer night. |
| August 6 | "I was listening to something I heard before." |
| August 7 | Someone is calling your name. |
| August 8 | Write about something that was stolen. |

1. Make a commitment to yourself to finish the piece no matter what. Even if you know it won't be perfect and it isn't what you intended to write. Make the commitment, then hang in there. (Better make a deadline for yourself, too.)

2. Promise yourself a reward for finishing. Make it a something you value, something you've been wanting for a long time. Absolutely give it to yourself when you complete the project. Make a big production out of it. (We know this is bribery. Do it anyway. You deserve it.)

■ You do great on synopsis or outline, but can't get into the full-out writing of the piece.

*All good writing is built one good line at a time. You build a novel the same way you do a pyramid. One word, one stone at a time, underneath a full moon when the fingers bleed.*

*— Kate Braverman*

1. Instead of writing the synopsis or outline, just start right in on the writing. Could be you're tired of the thing before you've even written it. There's nothing to learn, no surprises.

2. When you tell the story the way you think it should be told, you rob the story of the opportunity to tell itself. "I write to find the story," says novelist Wally Lamb. Don't worry that you don't know what the piece is about; just write and let the "aboutness" appear.

■ You are intimidated by the idea of writing a long, sustained piece whether "long" means a 1,500-word essay, a 5,000-word story, or a 300-page novel.

1. Write in short bursts, a paragraph at a time, just one scene. Anne Lamott calls these "short assignments." Don't consider the distance between beginning and ending; just write today's assignment.

2. Set a goal of a page a day, or 400 words a day, or set a time limit: twenty minutes, an hour. Make your goals or time limits manageable. Do it a day at a time.

■ You continue to edit and rewrite the same piece or the same section over and over, never adding any new material or starting anything else.

1. Put the materials you've already written (and rewritten) away. Work only on new material without any rewriting, writing only in your notebook. Don't enter any of it into the computer and don't go back and edit the previous day's writing. Do this for a month. Don't worry about the rawness of it. You can clean it up later. Just keep writing.

....................................................................................

■ You attend workshop after workshop, taking the same old material out for another go-around of read-and-critique, but you never write anything new or incorporate the critique you received. Or, you keep sending much-rejected pieces out to different publications.

1. Try the suggestion listed under the preceding "stuck" description. And remember this old adage: Writers write.

2. Instead of signing up for another workshop, spend the time you would be at the workshop writing new material. If part of what you love about being at a workshop is being in a new place and interacting with other writers, invite a writing friend to go away on a retreat with you. *(See Beyond Practice — Writing Retreats.)*

3. If you've sent the same piece out more than a dozen times without rewriting any of it and all you've gotten is rejections, consider that (a) you may be sending it out to the wrong markets or, more likely, (b) you need to take another look at it and do some rewrites.

■ You talk about writing all the time, but you don't put pen to paper.

1. Sign up for a class or workshop where group exercises are part of the process and homework is assigned.

2. Make writing dates with friends, do the topic of the day together. *(See Beyond Practice — A Writing Date.)*

■ You make writing dates with yourself but you don't keep them.

1. Include a friend on the date. It's easier to show up if you know someone is expecting you.

*If you write a hundred short stories and they're all bad, that doesn't mean you've failed. You only fail if you stop writing.*

— Ray Bradbury

| | |
|---|---|
| August 9 | On the other side. |
| August 10 | I've never seen his face. |
| August 11 | This is what the neighbors saw. |
| August 12 | Write about something that made you cry. |

2. Change the appointment to a time that works better for you — if not morning, lunchtime. If not lunchtime, right after work. Make your dates very brief — ten or fifteen minutes. Anyone can write for ten or fifteen minutes.

■ You often sign up for classes or groups, but drop out after a few sessions.

1. Know what's expected of you before you sign up. If one of the requirements is to bring six or eight or ten pages of work every session, make sure you have the time and are willing to commit to the workload.

2. Commit to being part of the group and showing up each time. If you're having difficulties, talk it over with the instructor or group leader rather than simply dropping out. Be willing to ask yourself the real reasons why you stopped attending. 🐾

*I started to discover I was being more honest when I was inventing, more truthful when dreaming.*

— Michael
　Ondaatje

## How to Get Unstuck

Still stuck? Try some of these ideas on ways to get rolling again.

1. Take a walk.
2. Take a shower.
3. Take a long, luxurious bath, with music, candles, and bath salts.
4. Wash the dishes. Or work in the yard. Sweep the porch.
5. Take a nap.
6. Try starting again (from a different place, point of view, time, setting).
7. Rewrite what you wrote before.
8. Copy pages of someone else's writing. Especially a writer you adore.
9. Kick around your ideas with someone else, maybe someone who isn't a writer.
10. Get in a writing group.
11. Change your place of writing (get out of the house, stay home, go to a café).
12. Change the time of your writing.
13. Change your clothes.
14. Set a deadline (a page a day, a scene by tomorrow, rough draft by Tuesday).
15. Remove a deadline.

16. Use freewriting, stream of consciousness, write nonsense.

17. Write your favorite words, then make sentences with them, then paragraphs.

18. Go to a poetry reading, just to listen.

19. Listen to music. Make music.

20. Go to a museum, a gallery. Look at art. Make art.

21. Read poetry aloud or listen to poetry or spoken word tapes or stories on tape.

22. Read a book you've been meaning to read. Reread a favorite.

23. Take a long, literary breath. Write a single sentence for seven minutes or longer.

24. Write in your journal.

25. Meditate.

26. Go to the movies, rent a video (create your own film festival of a favorite star or director or screenwriter or writer).

27. Work on another project (writing or otherwise).

28. Write a letter to someone describing your problem.

29. Let the piece cool off. Come back to it in a few weeks or months.

30. Notice the details. Look out your window and write what you see.

31. Start with one concrete detail and follow where it leads.

32. Plant some flowers. Work in the garden.

33. Light a candle, say a prayer, request a dream. ❧

*Talent isn't enough. You need motivation — and persistence too: what Steinbeck called a blend of faith and arrogance.*

— Leon Uris

| | |
|---|---|
| August 13 | And when autumn finally arrived. |
| August 14 | Write about the careless days. |
| August 15 | Aftershocks of the full moon. |
| August 16 | "Sleeping Where I Fall." (after Peter Coyote) |

## Writers and Their Day Jobs

**Hans Christian Andersen** worked in a tobacco factory at age eleven.

**Jack London** worked in a cannery at age thirteen.

**Charles Dickens** pasted labels on bottles of shoe polish.

**Carl Sandburg** was a firefighter, a traveling salesman, and secretary to the mayor of Milwaukee.

**E. B. White** sold roach powder and played the piano.

**Zane Grey** was a dentist.

**William Carlos Williams** was a doctor.

**Wallace Stevens** was a lawyer for an insurance company.

**Mona Simpson** worked as an ice cream scooper, a waitress, a stock clerk, a Christmas present wrapper, a neurophysiology lab assistant, a movie theater usher, an acupuncturist's assistant, and an editor.

**Alice Munro** picked tobacco while a university student.

**Carson McCullers** put in time as a waitress and played the piano for a dance class.

**Colette** supported herself by performing in a music hall, writing theater reviews, and, briefly, running a beauty salon.

**Christopher Marlowe** moonlighted as a counterespionage agent investigating English Catholics abroad.

**Erich Maria Remarque** sold tombstones and played the organ in an insane asylum.

**Raymond Carver's** day job was a night job: he worked as a janitor.

**Milan Kundera** worked as a laborer and a jazz musician.

**Daniel Defoe** was a spy and spin doctor for the Tories and the Whigs.

**William Burroughs** was an anthropologist and a private investigator.

**Isaac Asimov** compiled encyclopedias and taught chemistry.

**Christopher Isherwood** served as secretary to a violinist.

*You must not suppose, because I am a man of letters, that I never tried to earn an honest living.*

— George Bernard Shaw

T. S. Eliot was a banker.

Philip Larkin was a librarian.

Russell Banks was a plumber.

Mark Jacobson was a cabdriver.

Richard Farina was a songwriter.

May Sarton worked during the war years for the Office of War Information, where she wrote documentary film scripts.

Walt Whitman was a typesetter, a journalist, an itinerant schoolteacher, and a newspaper editor.

Herman Melville was a customs inspector for the New York Harbor Authority.

Anthony Trollope was a civil servant for the postal authority and is credited with inventing the letter box.

William Faulkner served as postmaster for the University of Mississippi post office.

Hart Crane was a factory worker in Cleveland.

Alex Haley spent twenty years in the U. S. Coast Guard.

Maya Angelou worked as a cook and managed a restaurant.

Among others, E. L. Doctorow, Mary McCarthy, Toni Morrison, William Styron, Gore Vidal, Lisa Alther, John Ashbery, Rick Moody, Amy Clampitt, and Dorothy Parker worked in publishing. ❧

The Writing Life

| | |
|---|---|
| August 17 | Nothing has changed. |
| August 18 | At the other end of the street. |
| August 19 | Write about the silent treatment. |
| August 20 | Write about stealing time. |

## Hunting and Gathering

Like our ancestors, writers go beyond the familiar and safe confines of home for those things that feed and clothe our work; no one will bring them to us. It's necessary and it's also a grand adventure.

Though it is possible to write wildly and imaginatively without ever leaving home (Emily Dickinson in her white room; Marcel Proust beneath his covers), most of us must go "out there" to experience the world, to interact with other people, to take our senses on a field trip; to watch, observe, record, and harvest. On each excursion we fill our sacks with booty, then haul it home and spill it out on our writer's workbench.

Have some fun, go on hunting and gathering expeditions:

- Dress as your character and go out into the world as him or her. Observe and interact from his or her point of view.
- Imagine this is the last time you will venture out: you are dying, you are going to prison, you are moving away, you are withdrawing.
- Notice everything that is dying and how it is dying; notice everything that is new and fresh.
- Pay attention to everything that is yellow or green or red.
- Pretend you cannot read or cannot understand the language.
- What if you are deaf? Blind? Cannot speak?
- Act as if this is the first time you've been to this place. You are a foreigner, a visitor.
- Note that which is man-made and that which is natural. Notice attractions and rejections, confluences.
- Go to the same place at the same time every day for a few weeks or a month. Record what is the same, what is different.

*See Places to Practice, Fresh Images and How to Find Them, Write from the Senses*

*In every writer there is a certain amount of the scavenger.*

— William Faulkner

## Images That Haunt You

Close your eyes and an image appears behind your darkened lids; write in your notebook and your words take shape around the same, familiar vision. It appears and reappears, sometimes shape-shifting, sometimes merely disguising itself. Explorations of this recurring image might lead to a single piece or the idea could be symbolic of a major theme, the leitmotif of your writing.

"I think all writers have one thing that sticks with them, one sticking point, and they write their books over and over again until they've solved it," said novelist Anne Rivers Siddons.

For me, the "sticking" thing is women and children — an old woman finds a newborn in a Dumpster, a mother leaves her baby on a train, a woman runs away from home with her three daughters. Story themes continue to appear in different forms and I write them without knowing their significance. I may never know, but I trust my writing is teaching me something important or helping me to work through some issues on a deeper level.

My friend Dian writes about sisters, Michelle's theme is relationships gone awry, precocious children appear in many of Wendy's stories, and for James it's the adventurer on a quest.

Often, rather than a theme that surfaces, single images have haunted me until I wrote them. Stopped at a traffic light one afternoon, I spotted a woman high up on the balcony of a retirement home, watering plants. She wore a brilliant green dress and her silver hair glinted in the sunlight. An image of her free-falling down the side of the building suddenly appeared to me and, for three years, until finally I wrote the story, the image would not leave me be. (In

*You know what images are important because they hit you so powerfully. But you don't always know what they mean.*

— Gloria Naylor

| August 21 | Write about an overheard remark. |
| August 22 | You picked up a hitchhiker. |
| August 23 | Something's burning. |
| August 24 | Write about being on the inside. |

my story, she didn't fall to her death, but instead landed in the swimming pool and floated to the top looking for all the world like a water lily in full bloom.) Other recurrent visions have been homeless men shouting at the sky and cowgirls in leather fringe riding trick ponies.

As an exercise, create a list of your recurring images, noting a few concrete details of each in a paragraph or so. For the next few practice sessions, expand on one of the pieces to see where it takes you.

You can trust these recurring images. Their resonance signifies a deeper connection, perhaps something that can never be clearly stated, something outside the cognitive and beyond language, a conjuration from that mystical place of spirit. Writing these echoing images will reveal you to yourself. This is one of the gifts of writing. ❧

*See Turn the Soil, Rereading Your Practice Pages, Discover What You Want to Write About*

## Writing about Real People

How will Aunt Thelma react when she reads what you wrote about her? Can your ex sue you for writing about his bad habits and bad breath? Writing about real people can be tricky; it can cause one set of problems as you write and a whole other set when the piece is published.

During the writing, you might be afraid to write about certain people because you're concerned you might hurt their feelings. You're scared you might reveal secrets or betray confidences. In this phase, the editor and censor are constantly on duty with their sharpened pencils and pursed lips, circling and pacing as you write. So you get stuck, or you write around something, or you hold back and the writing suffers.

But let's say you circumvented or outwitted or somehow evaded the editor and the censor and wrote something true about real people, something that might be looked upon by them as harmful and mean-spirited. And let's say this material got published. The problems that might arise from this scenario have to do with libel, and both you and your publisher could end up in a court of law.

For most of us, the first situation is far more common than the second. Even better, there are several ways to combat the first problem and most of them make the second problem moot.

In writing fiction, one sure way to avoid the psychological tangles that come from the feeling that you're exposing people and telling secrets is to disguise the real person as somebody else, somebody totally fictional, made up of bits and pieces of other people — a composite character. Right away you're guaranteed more freedom to fictionalize, and, knowing how characters like to take over

*Every person you meet — and everything you do in life — is an opportunity to learn something. That's important to all of us, but most of all to a writer because a writer can use anything.*

— Tom Clancy

| | |
|---|---|
| August 25 | Write about the morning after. |
| August 26 | Write about what has yet to happen. |
| August 27 | You are in the backyard. |
| August 28 | Write about a dangerous ride. |

stories, there might be some surprising turns of event you would have never included if you'd tried to stick to the "way it happened" with the real person.

Another technique to waylay the problem is to change enough facts that the real person would never recognize him or herself. Make her a him, give him more children or take some away, move the family from Cleveland to Boise, have the character drive a bus instead of sell insurance.

Truly fictionalize your fiction.

If you're writing nonfiction, you might consider asking the person's permission to include him or her in your piece, as memoirist Anaïs Nin did when she published her *Diaries*. Of course, if you're writing something that could be considered damaging to that person, or harmful, you probably wouldn't pursue this tack.

Another approach, and most common among autobiographers and memoirists, is to change some of the names or biographical facts, alterations that are disclosed in a disclaimer at the beginning of the book, or in the introduction.

In the end, there may be some people, minor characters perhaps, about whom you wrote — Aunt Thelma, for example, who did get her feelings hurt because you wrote about the time you got sick from her apple dumplings — who will experience hurt feelings and won't suffer them well. As a writer, this is a chance you take and a price you may have to pay. However, hurt feelings aren't libelous. To be libeled, a person must prove harm done and that, as a writer, you intended them harm.

Remember this: "If you have lived it, seen it, experienced it, or felt it, it's your story" and you have a right to tell your story any way you want. ❧

*See Family Stories, Transferring Real Life to Fiction, It's All Copy*

*... not every-thing happened to me, but the things that didn't happen seem true to me in a way that sometimes things that really did happen don't.*

*— Amy Hempel*

## Hot Nights/Wild Women (For Men, Too)

When was the last time you howled at the Moon? Dallied in erotica? Wrote about your skin and bones and wild imaginings? This writing session says do it Now. Do it when trees hang heavy with ripened peaches and heat shimmers the night sky. Do it when your writer's mind is restless and it's too hot to sleep. Surrender your pen to your outlaw self and write in the language of thunderstorms and sudden passion. Write in vibrant hues, the colors of the night — indigo, violet, the deepest shades of magenta. Put your ear to the ground and write its thrumming. Write your heartbeat, your blood song, the rattle and clack of your bones, the sizzle of air against skin. Write the geography of your soul, the map of your senses, the certain and electric poetry of your body. Write from your reckless mind and resonating memories.

This is what you do: Let loose your hair, your clothes. Unbind yourself. Go barefoot, go by yourself, go outside and into the night. Let the Moon be full and an untamed scent be in the air. Breathe it deep into your lungs and feel it beating against your ribs, then let it out in a long, sustained howl. Offer yourself up to the Moon and listen to the echo of your own yowling coyote song. You are wild woman, according to *cantadora* and writer Clarissa Pinkola Estes, "fluent in the language of dreams, passion, and poetry."

Under the night sky, beneath the Moon of new ripening corn, the Moon when cherries turn black, write in your notebook. Write 14 fruits you love to eat and 13 ways you like to eat them, list 33 ways you want to make love and 25 places you want to do it. Lie on your back in the grass and search out your own constellation in the sky. Say its myth. Sing and chant and dance to your own

| | |
|---|---|
| August 29 | My mother once told me … |
| August 30 | " … and her red hair lit the wall." |
| | (after Victor Hugo) |
| August 31 | "It's my belief we're all crazy." |
| | (after Trudy, the bag lady) |

night music. Name yourself wild woman or man and write your real name. Do it as an act of liberation. Stay up all night long, watch the stars wheel across the heavens, track their path on the pages of your notebook. Describe the colors of the sky, write its depth. At the darkest hour, gather wood and build a fire. Listen for the dawn.

More suggested topics:

- In the heat of the night.
- This is where I come from.
- Write about the full moon.
- Write about a time you made love.
- My body is ...

# SEPTEMBER

"Write in recollection and
amazement for yourself."

—Jack Kerouac

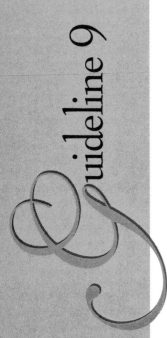

## Write Accurate Details

Writing accurate details doesn't mean your writing has to be factually true, but the specificity of detail is what brings your writing to life. The truth isn't in the facts; it's in the details.

"The more detail that you give to the reader, the more you help their imagination," said National Book Award winner Charles Johnson. It matters little what kind of sandwich you actually ordered during that lunch when your lover broke up with you, but if you say you were eating a grilled cheese or, for irony's sake, let's make it a hero or maybe turkey sandwich, the moment becomes more alive and real for the reader. They can taste that turkey and mayo on sourdough and how a mouthful of tears affects it. Rather than bird, write sparrow or starling; instead of tree, write eucalyptus or willow. Be specific with details that are true and right for the piece. Don't bloom your azaleas in the fall or pop up your toast before Herbert Hoover was elected. Research, if you need to, for accuracy.

Of course, you can go overboard and use so many details that reading your piece is like slogging through seaweed. Choose your details carefully, use the most telling ones. "I try to go for the detail that lights up in me like a neon light," said Spalding Gray.

Specificity is generosity, someone once said. So, notice what you notice — especially through your five senses — and write it down.

## Family Stories

Everyone has family stories. In many ways they are all the same and at the same time, all different. "I could write a book about my crazy family," people say. And indeed, most of us could. Southern writer Flannery O'Connor said that if we survived childhood we have enough material to last a lifetime.

Family stories in and of themselves — the verbatim of what happened to who — are not often the stuff of great literature, but that doesn't mean they shouldn't be written. Many people choose to write a family history or autobiography just to share with the family. The 1990s were the age of the memoir and the "new autobiography," as diarist and writer Tristine Rainer named it in her book of the same title.

Writing family stories does more than recollect times gone by, it celebrates what is grand and grieves what needs to be grieved; this is one of the ways we heal. Whether you want to write your autobiography or simply use your family memories as grist for your writer's mill, here are some exercises that can help you plumb for stories rich with detail, and find the truth.

■ Use the "I remember ... " exercise described on page 202. Begin with "I remember my mother ... " or "I remember my father ... " or use the name of another family member.

■ As suggested by poet Steve Kowit in his book *In the Palm of Your Hand*, begin with a series of dates such as "Summer, 19__," and write a memory, then list another date, or begin with the phrase: "The year I turned eight, the year I turned sixteen," and so on. Be sure to use the same intuitive, spontaneous writing that is used in the "I remember ... " exercises.

*Some people don't really bother much with remembering; it seems such a useless activity. But most writers are addicted to it.*

— Alice Munro

## Writing Topics

| September 1 | Write a December memory. |
| September 2 | "It was Sunday morning." (after Sharon Olds) |
| September 3 | Write about your neighborhood at 5 P.M. |
| September 4 | You eavesdrop on a conversation. What do you hear? |

TIP
OF THE
MONTH

*When you walk into a room and you get a certain feeling or emotion, remember back until you see exactly what it was that gave you the emotion. Remember what the noises and smells were and what was said. Then write it down, making it clear so the reader will see it too, and have the same feeling you had.*

— Ernest Hemingway

■ Sketch a floor plan of the house you grew up in, then write about each of the rooms. As you describe them, bring forth memories of being in those rooms, alone and with other family members. Remember to use specific details, drawing upon your senses.

■ Create a map of your neighborhood, write what it was like in the spring or winter, or at eight o'clock in the morning or three in the afternoon. At night. Write the trees and the houses, the streets and fences. Look in your neighbor's windows.

■ Write about holidays. Family gatherings, special occasions. Remember your birthdays and how they were celebrated. Sit everyone down at the dinner table and re-create a meal together.

■ Do character sketches of members of your family. Free-write for ten or twelve minutes. Go beyond physical characteristics and include attitudes, beliefs, habits and quirks, manner of speech, maybe some dialogue. Include the three aspects of any character: physical, psychological, and social. Use lines like: Uncle George was the kind of man who … then list four or five attributes.

■ Imagine you're watching your mother. Write what you see.

■ List some habits of your father.

■ Write about comings and goings. Who left, who stayed.

■ Make a list of the smells of your grandmother's bedroom, your parents' car, the back porch. List the sounds you heard in the morning when you awoke, what kept you awake a night. Use other sense lists as a way of entering memories.

■ Write a collection of firsts: First day of school, first date, first kiss, first time you saw blood, first funeral, first book you read, first time you thought differently than your mother or father, first time you were scared.

■ In your mind's eye, create a photograph of your family posed together. Notice who's leaning into whom, who's touching, where hands are placed and eyes are focused. Look into the faces, write what you see. Write what happens right after the photo is snapped. ✺

*See Transferring Real Life to Fiction, Writing about Real People*

## Clichés and Other Bad Habits

Clichés, like petty crimes and faux pas, are often committed without thought. "First thought is best in Art, second in other matters," said the poet William Blake. So the "first thought, best thought" dictum that works so well in evoking images and memories may not be the best source when it comes to word choice and creative phrasing. Either out of simple laziness or faster-than-light efficiency, when asked to "complete this phrase," the brain's best shot will be something as tired and mundane as brown shag carpeting. For example, just off the top of your head (there's a cliché for you), complete these phrases with your first thought:

*To write simply is as difficult as to be good.*

— W. Somerset Maugham

Soft as _____.
Dark as _____.
The clouds were like _____.
Hot as _____.
_____ as rocks.

You get the point.

What's a cliché? In talking to her journeyman writing class, a teacher once said, "For you, it's anything you've ever seen or heard before." Now try describing a mountain range or an ice cream cone.

Every writer commits clichés. One of the jobs of rewriting is to find these gravy stains on your necktie and clean them up. Also, the more aware you are of clichés, the less likely you are to use them. Here are a few tips to circumnavigate, levitate above, tunnel under, ride roughshod over, and generally avoid these bad habits.

| | |
|---|---|
| September 5 | The time between dusk and dawn. |
| September 6 | Write about a fragrance. |
| September 7 | Write about a place you long for. |
| September 8 | _____ is the color I remember. |
| September 9 | Write about a car trip. |

■ Read your writing aloud after every draft. Clichés stand out more clearly when they're spoken. The undiscerning eye sometimes sides with the lazy brain.

■ Go through and underline each suspect in a different ink color. Notice the frequency of usage. The more brightly colored your page, the more work you have to do.

■ Ask your writing partner to give you feedback. If your group hands out manuscripts for read-and-critique, have the readers mark clichés with a big "CL."

■ Don't settle for the first phrase you come up with; close your eyes and try to see the image more clearly. Write and rewrite.

■ Become cliché-conscious. Note their appearance in everything you read. Like a wary parent after curfew, the more sensitive you become the less likely they can sneak in unnoticed.

As the old saying goes, "avoid clichés like the plague." &

*See Auditioning Words, About Language, Better Verbs, Wordplay, When the Words Aren't Working — A Helping Hand*

*Writing above all, is seeing clearly.*

— Peter
    Matthiessen

## Stream of Consciousness and Other Intuitive Writing

What a great freedom to write stream of consciousness, to let the pen fly like a dervish while you hang on for the ride nabbing thoughts as they appear out of some wild, flamboyant place in your mind. Stream of consciousness and other intuitive writing is the magic carpet of writing techniques, producing funny, fantastic, surreal stuff, spoken in a language rich with imagery and musicality.

Called by many names — stream of consciousness, free-intuitive writing, flow writing, free association, automatic writing, spontaneous writing — this method of writing reaches into the deep recesses of the intuitive and brings forth words and ideas that can surprise and delight you. Use it to plumb for new images and ideas, to unstick yourself, to set a rhythm, to free your imagination, and, sometimes, just for the fun of it.

*The unconscious creates, the ego edits.*

— Stanley Kunitz

It's a simple technique, calling for nothing more than emptying your mind, then hopping on the back of any passing thought or image and riding it to the next, and then the next. André Breton, leader of the surrealist movement in Paris in the 1920s, suggested this:

"Attain the most passive or receptive state of mind possible. Forget your genius, your talents, and those of everyone else.... Write quickly with no preconceived subject, so quickly that you retain nothing and are not tempted to reread. Continue as long as you please."

When you use stream of consciousness writing, don't expect any logical sequence of thought. But do expect surprises. This technique delves into the innermost places of your subconscious; it can reveal thoughts, motivations, and desires. When images appear and reappear, the intuitive is giving you information. Pay attention.

September 10    Write about a time someone went too far.
September 11    I don't remember.
September 12    In a cemetery.
September 13    There's a bar in Austin, Texas, called "Jake's Place."
September 14    Write about someone who sinned.

## Quirks and Idiosyncrasies

**William Faulkner** loved the early 1960s TV program *Car 54, Where Are You?* Having no TV of his own, each Sunday night he watched it at a neighbor's home.

**Gustave Flaubert** kept his lover's slippers and mittens in his desk drawer.

**Alexandre Dumas**, the elder, ate an apple at 7 A.M. each morning under the Arc de Triomphe.

*Most writers are, at least, metaphysical outlaws anyway.*

— Tom Robbins

**Bjarati Mukherjee** will not leave the house if someone sneezes just as she's getting ready to leave and she doesn't cut her nails on certain days of the week.

**Anne Rivers Siddons'** husband reports that she makes a nest of papers, like a mouse getting ready for winter, then she starts walking into walls just before she begins a new novel.

**Stephen King** goes through these motions when he sits down to write: "I have a glass of water or I have a cup of tea. I have my vitamin pill; I have my music; I have my same seat; and the papers are all arranged in the same places."

Acquaintances recall **James Russell Lowell** removing and proceeding to eat with knife and fork a bouquet of flowers from the centerpiece at a literary supper in one of Boston's great houses.

**Gertrude Stein** scribbled her poems on odd scraps of paper in her Ford, "Godiva," parked at the curb. She had discovered her lofty position in the driver's seat was an inspiring spot in which to write.

It is alleged that **Henry David Thoreau** could swallow his nose. He also talked with forest animals. "I talked to [the woodchuck] in quasi forest lingo, baby talk, at any rate in a conciliatory tone, and thought that I had some influence on him."

As a child **Louisa May Alcott** wrote passionate letters to Ralph Waldo Emerson but she never sent them. She sat in the tall walnut tree in front of his house at midnight, singing to the moon.

**Charles Dickens** walked twenty to thirty miles a day. He also placed objects on his desk in exactly the same position, always set his bed in north/south directions, and touched certain objects three times for luck.

**Hans Christian Andersen** put a sign next to his bed that read "I am not really dead."

**Saint-Pol-Roux** hung the inscription "The Poet Is Working" from his door while he slept.

**Emily Dickinson** wouldn't see her dressmaker, go out of the house, or expose her handwriting. Her sister addressed all her letters.

Five years after *Nightwood* was published, **Djuna Barnes** left Paris, gave up smoking and drinking, refused interviews and photographs, and removed all the mirrors from her apartment.

**Shirley Jackson** owned more than 500 books on witchcraft.

At his funeral, **Langston Hughes** had arranged for a jazz trio to play "Do Nothing Till You Hear From Me."

And a few citings of sartorial eccentricities:

**Edgar Allen Poe** always wore black; **Emily Dickinson** only white; **Mark Twain** also attired himself in white, with shirts he personally designed that buttoned down the back. **Carl Sandburg** sported a green eyeshade when he worked, and **E. B. White** tied on a surgical mask in public to protect himself from contagious diseases. **John Cheever** donned his only suit of clothes when he went to his studio in the morning. He hung it up while he worked in his underwear, then dressed and returned home. **Allan Gurganus** said he wears a moving man's zip-up uniform because "I perspire so freely that I sweat my way through the fiction." **Forest McDonald** is said to write history on his rural Alabama porch — naked. ❧

| | |
|---|---|
| September 15 | "For as long as she lives, and probably longer, she will never forget his face." (after Alison Moore) |
| September 16 | Write about something you would do differently. |
| September 17 | Write about a purchase. |
| September 18 | It's raining now. |

# When the Words Aren't Working — A Helping Hand

You're going to have days like this: you reread your writing and discover you've used the same word three different times in the same paragraph. And it's not even a good word. It's a boring, mundane word. Worse, the only verb that attempts any movement at all is something past tense and lethargic: *was*. A snail of a word, taupe and gray in the middle of your sidewalk of a sentence.

You need help.

It's on days like this when you can be thankful to Messrs. Webster and Roget and others like them who made dictionaries and thesauri. These generous, helpful books can be your inspiration and your guides. They can show you the way to words you forgot you knew and words you never knew existed. Get big, jumbo-sized reference books and keep them within easy reach. Dictionaries and thesauri, language books that give you the origin of words and phrases. Dive into them just for the fun of it. Liven up your writing and increase your vocabulary at the same time.

I once worked for an editor who would not abide the use of a thesaurus. "If you don't know the word, you can't use it," he growled. But, oh, how I loved my Roget's. (I use J. I. Rodale's *The Synonym Finder* now, after years of using Sisson's *Synonyms*.) Late at night, when the candle flickers and I'm hanging on by my teeth to meet a morning deadline, and I give my manuscript one last edit only to discover I have used the word *gift* four times on one page, how grateful I am for my thesaurus when I can look up gift and find *present, favor, legacy, bounty, offering, blessing*, and nearly forty other synonyms that my weary brain could not locate in its on-line dictionary.

At a weekly read-and-critique session, one writer makes a list of all the words she hears that she doesn't know. When she gets home, she looks them up in her dictionary and tries to use them in her writing practice sometime during the next week. Others do this as they read, always keeping pen and paper nearby.

You can create your own stash of words in your notebook, too; mini dictionaries and thesauri customized for specific areas you're writing about.

*See Wordplay, Better Verbs, About Language, Writer's Notebooks, Auditioning Words*

*Easy reading is damned hard writing.*

— Nathanael West

## Practice Accoutrements

Though some say the best view for writers is a blank wall, the less outside stimulation the better, others believe in seducing the Muse with evocative accessories. Each writer gets to find his or her own way and whatever works is good. After all, Schiller had his rotten apples. If you're one who likes to arouse the creative with embellishments, following are some accoutrements other writers have brought into play.

*Music has often created the wellspring out of which my imaginative efforts have sprung.*

— William Styron

- Music, especially the classics: Mozart, Bach, Haydn, but jazz, too, or fusion, the so-called new age. Rock and roll if you've got the stamina, and blues if that's what it takes.
- Scents and Aromas: With so many aromatherapy scents to choose from, you can create a cacophony of odoriferous atmospheres. Think, too, of natural scents: a bowl of oranges, fresh rosemary, sprigs of pine or eucalyptus, bouquets of flowers. Wear your character's signature cologne as you write. Light incense, brew coffee, burn sage.
- Photographs and Postcards: Whether they remind you of the place you're writing, or are simply stimulating to look at, photographs stir the creative. Look beyond what you see for the smell and feel of the place or the people. (A great place to hunt down old photography and art books are used bookstores or Goodwill or Salvation Army stores.)
- Poetry: Read some poetry before you begin writing, or listen to spoken word tapes or CDs of poetry. Take a break from your writing and read a few poems or use a line or image from a poem to write from.
- Objects: Bring objects to your practice session — a seashell to explore and

September 19   Write about a time someone lost control.
September 20   Accept loss forever. (after Jack Kerouac)
September 21   Write a daydream.
September 22   "In the blue night frost haze ... " (after Gary Snyder)

name, an amethyst with its miniature purple mountain range, a fan from Bali, weeds from the garden, snail shells, locust carcasses, gumdrops, BBs, buttons, postage stamps. Make a collection of objects that you store in a basket on a shelf. Reach into it and surprise yourself.

■ Clothing: Dress as your character, dress as the opposite gender, wear someone else's clothes, slip into something you would never wear: a feather boa, a flowered housedress, or wedgies, for crying out loud. Work in your pajamas, your underwear, silk lingerie. ◈

*See The Writing Life — Invoking the Muse, Saying Yes to the Muse, How to Create a Space of Your Own*

# Find Your Tribe —
# Why Hang Out with Other Writers

Unlike your family and some of your friends, other writers don't think it odd that you talk about your characters as if they were actually alive. Other writers understand why you stay up half the night hunched over your computer, muttering to yourself. They know about the elusiveness of language, endings that won't come; they recognize the restlessness that comes with getting stuck in plot breakdowns. They also know the exhilaration of completing a chapter, a poem, or a short story because they experience it, too.

Hanging out with other writers is more than talking shop. It's different than a couple of fans sharing a beer and a game. Writers have always sought the company of other writers; there is a hunger for a connection that goes beyond the jargon and lingo and gossip of the trade. Call it psychic if you will, some kind of energy that vibrates at a sympathetic rate; something tribal and deep.

We are a species that gathers into community, not just we the writer species, but we the human species. Within these communities, we look for others who are like us. We form subcommunities and sub-subcommunities. When we are our best, we are inclusive and open. At our worst — when we operate out of fear — we become exclusive and protectionist. Ideally, what we are looking for is both safety and freedom. The freedom to be who we are without pretensions or alibis, and the feeling of being safe in expressing who we are.

As a writer, when you're with your own kind your writing is taken seriously, there is respect for the work that goes unspoken; no need for explaining or proving yourself. Within this circle there is an understanding that writing isn't

*The impulse for much writing is homesickness. You are trying to get back home, and in your writing you are invoking that home, so you are assuaging the homesickness.*

— Joan Didion

September 23   Write about a time someone surprised you.
September 24   Write about a door key.
September 25   Write about a simple pleasure.
September 26   Night is falling. You're not at home.

about being published or making money or becoming famous; no need to justify how much time you spend on a piece of work that may never see print.

Author and creativity guru Julia Cameron said that creativity is a tribal experience and that "tribal elders will initiate the gifted youngsters who cross their path." Isn't it true that writers help one another? "Try this publication," they'll say or "Sure, I'll be glad to give your story a read through." I never would have found the courage to begin this book nor the stamina to see it through to completion were it not for the generosity and enormous support of my writer friends.

Of course, this connection doesn't happen among all writers. No matter what tribe you belong to there will always be some members that just fry your banana. But those close connections with your own kind, this is what home feels like. Find them and nurture them. It's crucial to your writerly health and well-being. It's soul food. &

*See How to Start a Writing Practice Group, Find Support for Your Writing Life*

# How to Tell When the Censor Is Present

The censor is a completely different species than the critic or editor. The censor is that mean-spirited, tight-lipped, righteous character with a shriveled soul who hangs out on your extreme right. The censor is afraid of everything but disguises its fear by pronouncing judgments. Crossed-out words; cramped, crabby little handwriting; and bland, noncommittal verbiage all smell like the censor, musty and vaguely rancid. Here's a list of warning signs that the censor may be having an influence on your writing:

*Follow your inner moonlight; don't hide the madness.*

— Allen Ginsberg

- rejecting the "first thought, best thought" image if it feels risky
- listening to the "you can't write *that*" dialogue in your head
- worrying that you might hurt someone
- wondering what "they" will think of you
- looking around to see if anyone is watching you write
- writing dialogue that is boring, with characters who sound like normal folks
- crossing out dangerous words, replacing them with safer words
- avoiding writing certain scenes or memories
- using vague, generalized, or trite descriptions rather than concrete, vivid, original writing
- stopping suddenly and taking another, safer track, or quitting altogether
- drifting into ambiguity
- feeling embarrassed as you write or upon rereading
- choosing not to read your writing aloud
- immediately closing your notebook after you've finished
- feeling guilty or ashamed, like you've done something wrong or bad
- leaving the group right after it's over and not returning to the group after a particularly vulnerable session
- abandoning your writing completely for periods of time

Try as I might, there's nothing good I can find to say about the censor. If I had my way, I would pair up censorship with perfectionism and send them off hand in flinty hand to the boneyard.

*See Avoiding the Truth, Top Ten Fears of Writers, Take Risks*

# When Your Writing Embarrasses You

I know a woman who, when she was twenty-five, burned everything she'd ever written and she'd been writing half her life. Seeing herself so exposed on the page made her too uncomfortable; she was unable to separate herself at twenty-five from the passionate, angst-ridden fifteen-year-old whose writing was clumsy and naive. Or the eighteen-year-old who composed rhyming, sentimental poetry. She thought her writing was herself.

Sometimes in writing practice, you will lose yourself to the page and you won't be conscious of what you are writing. When you finish, you may feel as if you have been transported to another place and time, and maybe you have been. Reading what you've written may embarrass you because it reveals and exposes you, because it's so bad or because it's so unfalteringly good, because you wrote about your wildness and damaged the paper with all that raw energy.

"The best writers reveal something about themselves that a smarter person would choose to hide," said writer and editor Ken Foster.

Remember this: Your writing is not you. It is an expression of you that sometimes comes from a deep, unconscious place. And just as from time to time you have thoughts you cannot believe came from your mind — tearing the tongue from a sassy two-year-old, for example, or ravishing a stranger in a restaurant — what you write may be shocking, surprising, or downright embarrassing. "That came from me?" you say, incredulous. This is when you reach into your tool belt and pull out your sense of humor. When a shrug of self-acceptance rolls your shoulders and you shake your head at your wild mind and audacious imagination.

To be a writer is to be vulnerable to your art; to be a courageous writer is to do it anyway.

*See Being Vulnerable on the Page, Take Risks, How to Tell When the Censor Is Present, If You Want to Write (especially no. 6)*

*You have to be immensely daring, very skilled and imaginative, and willing to tell everything on yourself.*

— Raymond Carver

· · · · · · · · · · · · · · · · · · · · · · · · · · · · · · · · · · · · · · · · · · · ·

## Writing Marathon

I first read about writing marathons a number of years ago in Natalie Goldberg's book *Writing Down the Bones*. Over the years, I've staged many a marathon — from four to twelve hours or more. Seasonal marathons and Pre-Holiday Marathons, Late Night Marathons and Pizza Parties, Happy Hour Marathons, Write in the New Year Marathons, and the record-setting Blazing Typewriters Fundraising Marathon.

Marathons are not a test of creative endurance. They are a way to immerse yourself in your writing, to tread new ground, experiment, explore, take some chances, maybe break through barriers and let the words fall where they may.

Make your marathon as long as you want — half a day to all night long. Experience shows that half a day leaves writers wanting more and beyond twelve hours wears them out and makes them more than a little wonky.

Here's how it works: Gather together a bevy of writers, five to fifteen, for a set amount of time. Create a comfortable writing space. Provide all the prompts yourself or invite each writer to bring a prompt. Working with a variety of topics and accoutrements will keep the proceedings lively. Use the same guidelines for your marathon that you use for writing practice.

Among the prompts I have found to be effective are: collections of commonplace items that writers can choose from; color themes such as everything in red, or "going for the gold"; postcards, some of places and another set made up of people for which monologues are created; photographs cut from books; maps; boxes that contain items; sensory prompts that can be smelled, tasted, touched, and listened to; music; jewelry; personal items (participants remove

Beyond Practice

| September 27 | Write about a time the lights went out. |
| September 28 | Write about a time you did something out of superstition. |
| September 29 | The night won't save anyone. |
| September 30 | Write about a rendezvous. |

something they're wearing and put it in the center of the table). Also effective are interactive prompts that participants help create. For example, everyone writes a secret on a slip of paper, folds it, and tosses it in the prompt basket, or one person writes the first name of a character, the next writes a last name, the third, a telling detail, the fourth writes a monologue for this character.

Set different writing times for the topics. Begin with seven or ten minutes, work up to fifteen or eighteen, even thirty, then back down again. Invite readings after each writing, though with a large group not everyone will be able to read each time. Take breaks every one and a half to two hours.

Other tips: Provide nibbles and snacks, like fresh veggies and fruit. Of course, most writers I know like to lay on the sweets, too. Red licorice was a surprising hit. Include plenty of water and a meal break if your session lasts more than half a day.

After a marathon writers will probably be a little off balance. Spending even four hours in that deeper, intuitive space that writing leads can leave us on another plane. Grounding exercises and physical reentry of some kind can help rebalance participants. Expect dreams.

Some topics, just in case you need them:

- This is what my bones kept saying.
- She was the kind of woman who …
- Write about a progression of events.
- I live in _____.
- Write about Saturday night.
- These are the things you can trust.
- Write about a small disappointment.
- Skin.

*Don't be afraid of giving yourself away for if you write you must. And if you can't face that, better not write.*

— Katherine
    Anne Porter

# OCTOBER

"One of the few things I know about writing is this: spend it all, shoot it, play it, lose it, all, right away every time."

—Annie Dillard

## Write What Matters

If you don't care about what you're writing, neither will your readers. This doesn't mean you should take on only big subjects — war, peace, love, hunger, oppression. It means that if what matters to you is the way the light falls on the bougainvillea in the morning, that's what you should write about. If what matters to you is the relationship between sisters and brothers, then that's what you write about.

Write about what interests you, what you don't understand, what you want to learn more about. Novelist Amy Tan said, "I write about it (mothers and daughters) because I don't understand it, because it is such a mystery to me. If it ceases to be a mystery, and if I were an expert on it, I wouldn't write about it. I like to write about things that bother me in some way, that I have a lot of conflict with."

Reread your writing to discover recurring themes and images. Look for hints and innuendos within spontaneous or stream of consciousness writings. If you're bored with what you're writing, or lackadaisical about your commitment, return to the idea that birthed it. More than one writer has been drawn off track by comments from her writing group or misdirection from a friend. "Let nobody, your mother, your grandmother, your agent, your publisher, your producer, let nobody tell you the creator what you should do," said *Roots* author Alex Haley, who invested twelve years in writing his life-changing book.

Be a passionate writer.

. . . . . . . . . . . . . . . . . . . . . . . . . . . . . . . . . . . . . . . . . . . . . . . . .

## What Do I Do with All These Pages?

Once you start writing on a daily basis, the pages will pile up. You'll fill notebook after notebook with bits and pieces from practice sessions. What do you do with all this writing?

You may feel it's just practice, not worth saving, and set your notebooks out at the curb every Tuesday for recycling.

On the other hand, you may want to save every sentence, every paragraph, every practice session, even if you never look at the notebooks again. (Let your biographers have a fling with them when you're old and famous.)

Writers who use the practice sessions for filling in stories, novels, or essays may take one day a week to keyboard all the handwritten entries into the computer for editing and may not want to keep the notebooks after that.

Some may want to reread the entries once a month and tag those pieces for transplanting that might take root in a different setting.

One writer kept all her practice notebooks for a year then packed them up in boxes and took them with her on a month-long retreat to find out what she'd written. (Remember, writing practice shows you what you want to write about; themes emerge from disparate and seemingly disconnected pieces.)

Sometimes, upon rereading, you'll find a topic that will spark you to write again, maybe even a continuation of the original piece. (Topics can be recycled; it's almost guaranteed that you'll write something different each time.)

In *Writing Down the Bones*, Natalie Goldberg said she considered building a solar house out of her old notebooks. At that time, she had a stack about five feet high. I know another writer who plants a tree each Arbor Day as a symbolic

*In a very real sense, the writer writes in order to teach himself, to understand himself, to satisfy himself. The publishing of his ideas, though it brings gratification, is a curious anticlimax.*

— Alfred Kazin

## Writing Topics

| | |
|---|---|
| October 1 | On the night train to _____. |
| October 2 | Write about never and always. |
| October 3 | Write about taking a detour. |
| October 4 | Three things my father told me. |

## TIP
### OF THE
### MONTH

*Advice to young writers?*
*Always the same advice:*
*learn to trust our own*
*judgment, learn inner*
*independence, learn to*
*trust that time will sort*
*the good from the bad —*
*including your own bad.*

— Doris Lessing

gesture to acknowledge all the paper she's used during the course of that year's writing practice. You may want to do the same, creating a ceremony and celebration with some writing friends as a way of honoring the planet and giving back. (Imagine in some few years, another writer sitting in the shade of the tree you planted, leaning against its sturdy trunk, writing in her notebook.)

What you do with all your notebooks may depend upon how often you move and whether or not you want to lug all those boxes around. Also, how much spare room you have in your current living space and whether you're basically a saver or a chucker. One thing's certain: your filled notebooks are a testament to your commitment to writing and the time you invested in your craft. So whatever you ultimately do with those old notebooks, acknowledge yourself for that. ❧

## Imagination and Other Surprises

Imagination has been described as an "uncontrollable, risky chimeralike animal." To let it free may be to invite danger. But oh, what a delicious danger. Imagination is the playground for make-believe and magic. At once childlike and mystical, imagination is the landscape of surprise.

"Imagination is as necessary to a novelist or short story writer as the spinning of webs is to a spider and just as mysterious," said author B. J. Chute.

Most writers' imaginations are self-starting and in perpetual motion. But if, from time to time, you need to refuel yours, here are some ideas.

*The imagination has resources and intimations we don't even know about.*

— Cynthia Ozick

- Give rein to your curiosity, ask questions, and wonder why.
- Observe accurately.
- Watch children play.
- Pay attention to your dreams.
- Read often, read quality, and read a variety of materials.
- Lie on your back in the grass and stare into clouds.
- Look at shadows, rather than what makes them.
- Close your eyes and listen.
- Say what things look like besides what they are.
- Create the lives of strangers.

Imagine, rather than think. Imagine, rather than problem solve. Imagine, rather than ponder. Unfocus, let loose, and imagine. Be like Nobel Prize recipient Isaac Bashevis Singer, who said, "My imagination has been overstimulated all my life by life itself."

See *How Can You Tell When Imagination Is Present?*

| | |
|---|---|
| October 5 | Write about a fragment. |
| October 6 | Write about small mistakes. |
| October 7 | You're in a café. |
| October 8 | Losing control. |
| October 9 | "_____ are my weakness." |
| | (after Pam Houston) |

## When Characters Appear

Don't be surprised when characters, whom you could never in a million years think up, choose your writing-practice notebook in which to make an appearance. Welcome them. Invite them back. Give them plenty of space to tell their story. Use the daily topics to write from their point of view. This is how stories and novels are born.

For example, if Tuesday's topic is "write a motel story," and some redheaded woman named Ruby shows up and wants to talk, listen to her. Next day, no matter what the topic, let Ruby tell it. Give her enough elbow room and she's bound to include some other characters. Invite them in, too; follow Ruby's lead and let the story and relationships unfold. Check in again the following day and see what these characters have been up to. Just start the writing with the daily topic or begin with something that appeared the day before that interests you. Keep writing and after a while you'll have some bones that you can cleave a story to. "The time will come when your characters will write your stories for you," said visionary writer Ray Bradbury, "when your emotions, free of literary cant and commercial bias, will blast the page and tell the truth."

Not every character who materializes through your writing practice is someone you'll want to stay with. They may be around for a while then the story will fizzle out on its own; you'll get bored or they will and the affair will end. You may never hear from them again or, at some later session, they'll reappear. "All writers have a cast of characters that keep turning up under different names and different sexes," said novelist Doris Lessing. "Sometimes these characters can surprise you; sometimes they go past so fast you often don't notice them."

Others won't leave you alone. Like my friend Amy, whose protagonist showed up at a writing marathon and, a year and a half later, she's still around recounting her story while Amy writes it all down. They're on their second draft now.

Working with characters is like dancing: sometimes you lead and sometimes they do. It's a matter of trusting your partner and listening to the music.

*See Use Practice as Building Blocks*

*I truly think that you can't go and stock your material, you have to leave the door open, and whatever chooses you, chooses you. You can't go and wrestle it to the ground.*

— Louise Erdrich

## Rereading Your Practice Pages

Rereading your practice notebooks after a period of time is like taking a trip to a place that is at once familiar and yet somehow different, like revisiting an old neighborhood. Some streets and buildings you'll remember exactly, but when did that house with the dormer windows get built and was that fence always leaning that way, ragged and a little dangerous? You may not remember how green this place was, how generous the trees.

Set aside an open-ended chunk of time; you won't want to rush the process. Gather several old notebooks, colored pens, and sticky notes and find a quiet place where you can lose yourself in the folds of your writing. It's best to read the notebooks in chronological order — there will be a natural building of pieces over time and recurrent writings, an organic unfurling of images; characters will reveal themselves over several sessions. You'll discover repeating themes and images, ideas tugging at your sleeve saying, *write me, write me.*

As you read, tag pieces for transplanting into other gardens. Use colored pens to mark reappearing themes. Transcribe lines, images, and descriptions to your writer's notebook lest they be lost to the pages of these practice notebooks. You may also find pieces that you want to continue in subsequent practice sessions or topics to write about again. Make notes of all this. At the end of a rereading your notebooks will look ragtag and earmarked and flapping like a ticker tape parade.

Without a doubt you will find junk, pages and pages of junk. You may find yourself yawning over pieces that bored you even when you wrote them. But you'll also find jewels you didn't know existed, traces of your brilliance scrawled on practice pages and gleaming there beneath the oblique light of slightly detached vision that can only come with time and distance.

> *I don't feel like a novelist or a creative writer as much as I feel like an archaeologist who is digging things up and brushing them off and looking at the carvings on them.*
>
> — Stephen King

| | |
|---|---|
| October 10 | "In those days, … " (after Roger Aplon) |
| October 11 | It was as far as I could go. |
| October 12 | Write a summer memory. |
| October 13 | Write about a pillow. |

## Quotas and Other Facts and Figures

**Thomas Mann,** working full time, wrote a page a day. He wrote every day.

For 25 years, **Gustave Flaubert** finished a big book every five to seven years.

**Jack London** claimed to write 20 hours a day. He set his alarm to wake him after four hours' sleep. But, because he often slept through the alarm, he rigged it to drop a weight on his head.

*I still have no way to survive but to keep writing one line, one more line, one more line …*
— Yukio Mishima

**Anthony Trollope** wrote 12 million words — 47 novels, 60 short stories, 40 pages per week, 250 words every quarter hour — he watched the clock. This made his friend **George Eliot** "quiver with dismay." Trollope, by the way, didn't start writing until he was 40. At age 67 he died of a stroke while laughing at the comic novel he was reading.

**Luigi Pirandello** vowed to write one short story for every day of the year. He still had 100 to go when he died.

A week before she died at 95, **Edith Hamilton** said, "You know I haven't felt up to writing, but now I think I am going to be able to finish that book on Plato."

**Paul-Toussaint-Jules Valéry** used to get up at five in the morning, work until nine, then spend the rest of the day having fun in one way or another.

**Emily Dickinson** wrote 1,800 poems, only seven of which were published in her lifetime.

**Anton Chekhov** wrote more than 300 short stories.

**Franz Kafka** completed *The Metamorphosis* in three weeks. An insurance agent by day, he confined his writing to weekends, nights, and vacations.

Historian **Shelby Foote** was reported to write 500 to 600 words a day — with a dip pen. It took him 20 years to complete his 1.5 million-word trilogy on the Civil War.

**Upton Sinclair** wrote 8,000 words every day including Sunday. In an 18-month period, while a full-time graduate student at Columbia, he wrote 1,275,000 words.

**William Saroyan** reported that after *Story Magazine* accepted "The Daring Young Man on the Flying Trapeze," he told them he would write one story every day for 30 days to illustrate the problem of writers who had no place to publish their work. On one of those days, he wrote three stories.

**Leo Tolstoy** rewrote *War and Peace* eight times and was still making corrections on the galleys.

**Donald Barthelme** wrote every day, seven days a week, and, he said, he threw a lot away. "Sometimes I think I write to throw away; it's a process of distillation."

**Eudora Welty** got up, got her coffee and an "ordinary breakfast," and went to work. At the end of the day, about five or six o'clock, she'd stop, have a bourbon and water, and watch the evening news.

**Tom Robbins** said he works five days a week, 10 A.M. to 3 P.M., with a goal of two pages a day.

**Joseph Wambaugh** said he writes 1,000 words a day, minimum, and if an emergency happens and he misses a day, he writes 2,000 words the next.

**Erica Jong** set herself to the task of writing ten pages a day in longhand, which comes out to about five typewritten pages.

**Rod Serling** spent about three hours a day writing. In terms of the prewriting activity, he said, "God, that's endless, it's constant."

**Tim O'Brien** said he puts in nine-hour days every day — birthdays, Christmas, Halloween — in part because "I love it so much." He also claims to be obsessive. ❧

The Writing Life

| October 14 | Write about being in a closed space. |
| October 15 | Write about promises made. |
| October 16 | You're driving in your car. |
| October 17 | When I opened my mouth to sing. |
| October 18 | Write about a hideout. |

## Writer's Block

Writer's block is one of those terms, like dysfunctional or codependent, that has been used to label so vast a range of symptoms that it's lost any real meaning. Not all interruptions of forward motion are writing blocks, just like not all behavior focused on another is codependent. Sometimes what might appear as a block is merely a pause in the action.

The farmer leaves the ground fallow for a season so it can regenerate itself. So, too, writers need to rest, to refill what has been emptied. Or a writer may be in a stuck place, simply needing a little push to get back to solid ground. Writer's block is a heavy term for such times as these, like using a sledgehammer when the tap of a ball peen would serve. By saying you're suffering from writer's block, you may scare yourself into something that's bigger than it needs to be.

Some writers don't believe in writer's block. Fiction writer Jamaica Kincaid said writer's block is just another part of writing, and editor Gordon Lish used the term "writer's search," rather than writer's block.

In her book *On Writer's Block*, Victoria Nelson wrote, "Although it can be triggered by any number of internal or external stimuli, the vital function that writer's block performs during the creative process remains constant: *inability to write means that the unconscious self is vetoing the program demanded by the conscious ego.*" In other words, it is not the block itself that is the problem, but the approach the writer is taking to the creative work.

Following is a list of potential causes and some solutions for an inability to write.

■ Look to expectations and perfectionism. The piece may not be emerging as you intended or even what you wanted. It's as foreign as an okapi. And not nearly as perfect.

■ Fear of failure, fear of success. Fear of finishing, fear of not being able to finish. Fear of any kind.

■ Some writers are as afraid of confrontation in their fiction as they are in their lives; this can cause problems in writing just as it does in real life.

■ Maybe the piece you're writing doesn't fit the mold you've chosen. Trying to fit a novel into a short story is like trying to limit a zucchini plant to zero population growth. Reshape the piece or change the mold.

*The way to find your true self is by recklessness and freedom.*

—Brenda Ueland

■ Trying to fit yourself into a mold, or conversely, to break out of one. Maybe you're the short story writer who longs to be a novelist, the nonfiction writer who thinks "real" writers write fiction, the children's story writer who believes it's time to mature into adult pieces. Rainer Maria Rilke advised, "One may do anything; this alone corresponds to the whole breadth life has. But one must be sure not to take it upon oneself out of opposition, out of spite toward hindering circumstances, or, with others in mind, out of some kind of ambition." In other words, attempt anything, but check your motives.

■ A sense of being overwhelmed. You're only 50 pages into your novel and you know you have at least 300 to go, plus all those rewrites. We're talking years. The enormity of this is daunting. Remember, writing happens word by word and novels get written scene by scene.

■ Examine lifestyle and work habits. Maybe you're trying to write when you're too tired or you're not getting enough rest or exercise. How's your diet? Too much caffeine, not enough fruits and veggies?

■ Take an inventory of other aspects of your life that may be causing stress or distraction. Illness, divorce or separation, job difficulties, relocation. Any of these can cause a temporary block. Now may not be the time to write. ⁂

*Rationality squeezes out much that is rich and juicy and fascinating.*

— Anne Lamott

October 19    Write about jealousy.
October 20    Someone says, "Can I see you in the kitchen?"
October 21    Write about a bruise.
October 22    I come from …
October 23    These are the lies I told you.

## The Most Human Art

## Ten Reasons Why We'll Always Need a Good Story
### By Scott Russell Sanders

1. We delight in stories because they are a playground for language, an arena for exercising this extraordinary power.
2. Stories create community. They link teller to listeners, and listeners to one another.
3. Stories help us to see through the eyes of other people. Through stories we reach across the rifts not only of gender and age, but also of race and creed, geography and class, even the rifts between species or between enemies.
4. Stories show us the consequences of our actions. To act responsibly, we must be able to foresee where our actions might lead; and stories train our sight.
5. Stories educate our desires. Instead of playing on our selfishness and fear, stories give us images for that which is truly worth seeking, worth having, worth doing.
6. Stories help us dwell in place. Stories of place help us recognize that we belong to the earth, blood and brain and bone, and that we are kin to other creatures.
7. Stories help us dwell in time. History is public, a tale of influences and events that have shaped the present; the mind's time is private, a flow of memory and anticipation that continues, in eddies and rapids, for as long as we are conscious. Narrative orients us in both kinds of time, public and private.
8. Stories help us deal with suffering, loss, and death. Stories reek with our obsession with mortality.
9. Stories teach us how to be human. We are creatures of instinct, but not solely of instinct. More than any other animal, we must *learn* how to behave.
10. Stories acknowledge the wonder and mystery of Creation. [They] give us hope of finding meaning within the great mystery.

*If there is magic in story writing, and I am convinced that there is, no one has ever been able to reduce it to a recipe that can be passed from one person to another. The formula seems to lie solely in the aching urge of the writer to convey something he feels important to the reader.*

— John Steinbeck

## The Discipline of Writing

*Discipline* comes from the Latin for teaching, learning. Discipline is about being a pupil, being teachable. "The discipline of the writer is to learn to be still and listen to what his subject has to tell him," said biologist and author Rachel Carson.

Discipline also means self-control. Writers need discipline — to be a pupil to their writing, to learn about it and from it; and they must have the self-control that will finally get the work done.

"Writing is as much discipline as it is desire," said novelist Christopher A. Bohjalian. "Don't wait until you're inspired, because if you do, you'll never finish anything."

Discipline means showing up at the page when you said you would. It means staying with a piece to completion, working through the problems as they arise, it means writing when you don't feel like writing or you're not "in the mood." Discipline is turning down invitations that interfere with your writing, and arranging appointments so that they mold around your writing time, not break it up.

When John Keats advised fellow poet Percy Bysshe Shelley to "curb your magnanimity," he wrote, "The thought of such discipline must fall like cold chains upon you, who perhaps never sat with your wings furled for six months together."

Discipline can be hard to come by. Writing isn't easy work. No art is. Staying with it as you slog through problems, as you face the blank page, as, word by word, you expose yourself on paper, can take every bit of self-control. A story

*What I did have, which others perhaps didn't, was a capacity for sticking at it, which really is the point, not the talent at all. You have to stick at it.*

— Doris Lessing

| | |
|---|---|
| October 24 | There is a place called _____. |
| October 25 | Write about small scrapes and bruises. |
| October 26 | Write about "what goes without saying." |
| October 27 | Write what the darkness proposes. |
| October 28 | "It was a summer of blue-black nights." (after Don DeLillo) |

circulated of one writer who tied the belt of his silk dressing gown to the arms of his chair just to keep himself at his desk.

All this doesn't mean discipline is a dirty word, some Ebenezer Scrooge that demands all of you and gives no quarter for fun or lightness or laughter. In fact, the opposite is true. Discipline is a loving act, returning to you the rewards of work completed — how else do you finish a 300-page novel, 120 pages of screenplay, a 3,000-word essay, except with the discipline of writing a page or a line or a word at a time? Discipline also gives you time without burden. Southern writer Eudora Welty said that when she'd finished her day's work, "I could do anything I wanted."

Being a writer, or any kind of artist, takes commitment and tremendous discipline. The great storyteller Charles Dickens wrote, "Whoever is devoted to an Art must be content to deliver himself wholly up to it and find his recompense in it." ❧

*See Daily Routine, Ten Daily Habits That Make a (Good) Writer*

*The most important thing for a writer is to be locked in a study....*

— Erica Jong

Beyond Practice

## A Walk in the Woods

It is fall, just past the equinox. The light has changed and tones are golden. There is a quieting now, a settling in. This is a good time to take your notebook for a walk in the woods. Go with a friend, if you like. Allow an easy morning or afternoon. Be prepared to slow down.

When you begin, walk for a long time, trying not to think, but to simply be. Walk not in order to arrive, but just to walk. "It is a great art to saunter," Henry David Thoreau told us. Pause when you will to examine the intricacies of a tree, its branches stretching up and out, the veins in a leaf, the tracks of a creature. No need for conversation. Better to walk in silence, to notice and observe. Listen to the symphony of the place, the play of sound against sound. Let the geometries of light lead you deeper into the woods, and the trail that you follow be the one less traveled.

"We need the tonic of wildness.... We can never have enough of nature," Thoreau wrote. He who "went to the woods because I wished to live deliberately, to front only the essential facts of life, and see if I could not learn what it had to teach, and not, when I came to die, discover that I had not lived."

Returning to the woods, to walk among the wild, refills a part of us we may not even know we have emptied. I have been witness to the tears of friends so moved by a feeling of homecoming they wept. I have experienced my own tears. It doesn't seem so strange to embrace a tree, to stand close and lean your body against its solid trunk, surround it with your arms, and press your cheek into its rough bark. Not so strange to wear dwindling flowers in your hair and encircle your wrists with vines. To be on hands and knees, tracking the trail of termites

October 29    "I'm at a loss ... "
October 30    "What will happen can't be stopped." (after Ann Beattie)
October 31    Write about someone who has passed to the other side.

into log, ants into rotting seedpod. To notice the backlit weave of spiderweb and sink into the soft mulch of earth. "You will find something more in woods than in books," wrote St. Bernard. "Trees and stones will teach you that which you can never learn from masters."

Finally, finally, find a place to sit, remove your notebook from your pack, and open to a blank page. Listen. Breathe in, and pause before you write.

The woods, the wild, the way the light falls and the air smells, topics surround you. Here are some more, in case you need them.

- Write an October memory.
- "A slight sound at evening lifts me up ..." (after Henry David Thoreau)
- Surviving twilight.
- This is what was left behind.
- Write about something out of the past.

# November

"If a writer is constantly concerned with truth, grace, order, and other verities, his inner life just naturally enriches in proportion to his working."

—William Saroyan

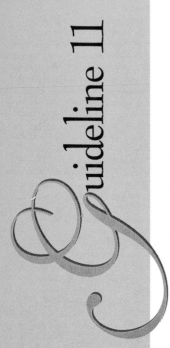

## Read Your Writing Aloud

After you've completed your writing session, read what you've written aloud to yourself or someone else. Reading aloud lets you know how your writer's mind works. It tells you when you're writing with authenticity and when you're telling the truth.

Reading aloud after writing practice isn't for feedback or critique of the work; it's too raw and unfinished for that. Rather, hearing it aloud allows you to experience the truth of a piece, to discover the depth of emotion it holds for you. And, because in writing practice you're working more from intuition than planning, you get to find out what you actually put down on paper. You get to hear your writer's voice.

Reading aloud serves other purposes, too. You hear the repetition in word usage as well as sentence structure. You pick up clichés and sense obstacles that might get in the way of the reader.

Best-selling novelist Allan Gurganus said, " ... there's a kind of ear music that operates as an editorial principle on the page even when a reader is not moving his or her lips. There's a kind of rhythmic [synchronicity] ... which somehow pulls them rhythmically into the fiction and creates a kind of heartbeat on the page."

To get started on the day's writing, novelist John Barth recommended you read aloud what you've written the day before. "It's to get the rhythm partly, and partly it's a kind of magic: it *feels* like you're writing, though you're not."

## Transferring Real Life to Fiction

Fiction writers have always used real life experiences as a source for material. In fact, any writer would be hard put to *not* include some of real life in his or her writing, and why shouldn't it be used? Most fictional fires start with real life sparking against imagination.

Whether primarily autobiographical or mostly imagined, all stories contain some of each element. Novelist Ann Beattie, who claims she's never written anything directly autobiographical, said, "at the same time I've never written anything that didn't honestly reflect some emotional state." Emotional honesty is the litmus test for successful fiction, and real life is the source for emotions.

Believability is another criterion. So even if "that's the way it really happened," some facts of real life simply won't play in fictional stories. Never mind that some of what we absolutely believe in fiction could never happen in real life. Or could it? Believability is about whether the events of the story or the behavior of a character ring true with the story as a whole.

Rearranging facts, compositing characters, altering time frames and locations, these are some of the ways to transfer the stuff of real life into fiction.

"I've always been a writer who has written from someplace reasonably close to experience," said Booker Prize–winning writer Salman Rushdie, "but it's always used, turned into something, put somewhere else, made something of."

*See Writing about Real People, It's All Copy, Truth versus Fact*

*A little autobiography and a lot of imagination are best.*

— Raymond Carver

## Writing Topics

| | |
|---|---|
| November 1 | Write about casting a spell. |
| November 2 | I dreamed _____. |
| November 3 | Write about yearning. |
| November 4 | The sun is rising. |

## TIP OF THE MONTH

*... rescue yourself from these general themes and write about what your everyday life offers you; describe your sorrows and desires, the thoughts that pass through your mind and your belief in some kind of beauty — describe all these with heartfelt, silent, humble sincerity and, when you express yourself, use the Things around you, the images from your dreams, and the objects you remember.*

— Rainer Maria Rilke

## Wordplay

Taking your writing seriously doesn't mean giving up the fun of it. Playing with words — squeezing out the sound of them, arranging them on the page in nonsensical visual dollops — is a delightful way to get some fun back into your work. When your writing begins to feel like manual labor under the August sun, lighten up with these playful tools.

■ Write the words you love (because of the way they look on the page, the way they sound) helter-skelter on a piece of paper. Play with the look of them. Make big loopy *L*s and round-as-a-baby's-tummy *O*s. Use colored pencils or pens. Or crayons. Don't think about which words to write; let your intuitive choose. In this exercise, the meaning of the words doesn't mean diddly. This wordplay activity is about the visual and aural qualities of the words. Each time you play with words, you'll come up with new loves. You're not fickle; you're expansive.

■ Choose one of your words and use it in a sentence. Now make another sentence with another word. Make a whole paragraph using your words. Read them aloud. Resonate with their sound, savor them in your mouth and as they pass through your ears.

■ See how many words you can come up with for a color, or a taste, or a sound. Try fifty words for the color orange, do twenty-five on drum, sixteen on sweet. Keep these in your notebook so you can refer to them.

■ Create your own thesaurus with these wordplay exercises. Make listings for the color of sky, the shape of clouds, the smell of rain; the contours of chins, noses, eyes; the sounds of laughter, crying, wonder, worry.

■ On index cards or construction paper (something thicker than plain printer paper), make a list of words, either by hand or on your computer, leaving enough space to cut them apart. Use nouns and verbs, a few adjectives. Make a word container out of a cool box or jar or basket. Place the cut-apart words in your container and mix them up.

Close your eyes and let your fingers find words to start you on a practice session. Select several to start a poem or create an image. Keep adding words to your word container and keep it nearby as you write.

■ In the midst of a practice session, dig into your jar of words for a word to use in your next sentence. Don't stop to look for a word, or think about how to use it … just go.

■ Poet Susan Wooldridge advised us in her book, *Poemcrazy*, to use manuals or reference books to find words. Mine car repair, home repair, woodworking manuals; look in field guides for birds of the Pacific Coast, Appalachian wildflowers, fly-fishing lures, bats, butterflies. Scour cookbooks, pottery books, sewing and glassblowing books.

■ Describe the way something sounds by using color words, write the way something tastes with mood words, use texture words or emotion words or taste words for the weather.

■ Clip words out of magazines and newspapers to make word collages.

■ Open the dictionary to any page and let your eye choose a word to prompt a writing session. Search out unusual words and say them out loud. Take turns with a friend to choose a page number, then find a word on that page to give each other for writing prompts.

■ In your portable notebook, list the words you notice in a day — on a walk, in a café, on menus, marquees, signs, bus boards, and billboards. These could be the beginnings of a found poem. List the words that find their way in through your ears as well as your eyes.

■ Ernest Hemingway wrote, "There were many words that you could not stand to hear and finally only the names of places had dignity." Write the names of

*A poem begins as a lump in the throat, a sense of wrong, a homesickness, a lovesickness. … It finds the thought and the thought finds the words.*

— Robert Frost

| | |
|---|---|
| November 5 | Write about divine intervention. |
| November 6 | You're eating breakfast. |
| November 7 | Secretly, I know my name is _____. |
| November 8 | Write about electricity in the air. |

places. Rivers and towns, rocks, plains, mountains, seas. Secret and sacred places of your own making, public places like beaches and baths, neighborhoods and hideouts.

■ Make a list of the jobs you've had and the verbs that describe the work you performed: hairdresser (wash, style, trim, cut, color, comb), cook (fry, sauté, chop, braise, roast), waitress, bank teller, lawyer, bartender, mechanic, woodworker, masseuse. Go beyond paying jobs to work you've done at home: painter (mix, stir, spackle, brush, stroke, roll, tape), gardener (dig, spade, plant, transplant, hoe, weed), chauffeur, cook, builder, bricklayer, nurse, seamstress, interior designer. ❧

## Where They Got Their Ideas

The idea for *Hay Fever* came to **Noël Coward** as he walked in a garden. He wrote it in three days.

**Katherine Anne Porter** said her writing began with an idea forming like a dark cloud. *Ship of Fools* began as notes in her journal and took thirty years to complete.

**Michael Ondaatje's** *The English Patient* drew on Count Almasy, the spy, but mostly the explorer. "I used the first part of his life then moved on into fiction."

In **John Barth's** book *The Floating Opera*, the floating showboat came from a photograph of an actual showboat he remembered from his childhood. It happened to be named *Captain Adams' Original Unparalleled Floating Opera*.

"Why Don't You Dance?" **Raymond Carver's** story, came from visiting writer friends in Missoula in the mid-1970s. Someone told a story about a barmaid named Linda who got drunk with her boyfriend one night and decided to move all her bedroom furnishings into the backyard. "They did it, too, right down to the carpet and the bedroom lamp, the bed, the nightstand, everything."

**Erica Jong**, who promised herself that she would write a Fieldingesque novel set in that period (eighteenth-century England), said the idea for her book *Fanny: Being the True History of the Adventures of Fanny Hackabout-Jones* really started with the simple question, What if Tom Jones had been a woman?

When **James Fenimore Cooper** included George Washington as a character in *The Spy*, it marked the beginning of his bid to render American history into epic form.

**Leo Tolstoy's** novel *Anna Karenina* had its origins in a newspaper story.

November 9    It's what I do at 2:30 in the morning when I can't sleep.
November 10   Write about where rivers join.
November 11   Write about a song you love.
November 12   This is what can happen when _____.

# How to Tell When Your English Teacher Is Present

When imaginary Rules of Composition and Grammar accompanied by prissy, righteous comments and precise little check marks surface between the lines on your page as if written in invisible red ink, you can almost hear your old English teacher *tsking* in your ear and smell her chicken-soup breath. (This isn't Glinda the Good Witch teacher who wrote "Great Imagination" in her generous hand-writing on your homework and laughed out loud at your stories. No, this is the Wicked Witch of the West teacher who drilled you in coordinate conjunctions, present progressive tense, who would not abide dangling participles, especially if they were past perfect.)

> *The necessity of the idea creates it own style. The material itself dictates how it should be written.*
>
> — William Faulkner

How do you know when your English teacher is present? Here's what to look for and how to get around it.

■ You worry over the structure of a sentence, rather than what it conveys.
(Say what you want to say, then clean it up later. Don't even worry if you're writing complete, proper sentences, at least not in practice.)

■ You're concerned about whether or not you've included all the elements of composition — the introductory paragraph with your thesis and how you're going to prove it, supporting paragraphs with specific examples, and a conclud-ing statement that restates your thesis.

(Don't get caught up in beginnings, middles, and endings. Just write. Let the piece stand on its own. "There is nothing to prove and everything to imag-ine," said absurdist writer Eugène Ionesco. You can rearrange, add to, and take from during rewrites.)

■ You get held ransom by a semicolon. Grammar flummoxes you.
(Don't worry about grammar or punctuation. Just write.)

■ All this talk about active vs. passive voice paralyzes you into no voice at all. Same with tenses — present, past, past perfect, it's got you all tensed up.

(It's not unusual for pieces composed during the intensity of writing prac-tice to be inconsistent in style and for time to travel from past to present and back again. Even names get changed and pronouns alter gender from one para-graph to the next. With practice, writers can train themselves to write in the active rather than the passive voice. Rewriting teaches. And with each piece you write and rewrite, you get to make any number of choices, including whether to use past or present tense. Listen closely as you reread your piece aloud; sometimes the tense that best suits the piece will appear.)

■ You're afraid to simply follow your pen. What if you clutter your paragraph with material that strays from your main point?

(Because it works in symbols and imagery, the intuitive mind connects the dots in ways that our thinking mind might never see. Let go and trust your pen. Sometimes the debris that is left in the wake of your wild mind turns out to be your main point.)

■ What you're writing doesn't seem to fit into any form you studied in school. When someone asks "what are you writing?" you don't know how to answer.

(Labeling work can stifle it, especially in its early stages. Let form come organically out of the work itself. When someone asks what you're writing and you don't know, it's okay to answer, "I don't know. It hasn't told me yet.")

■ The freewheeling idea of going outside the lines, using *all* the page with handwriting that looks as if it has a life of its own, is held in check by the nagging reminder: "neatness counts."

(When you hold back your handwriting you also hold back ideas. Just for the heck of it, open to a clean, unmarred page in your notebook and let 'er rip. Disregard the margins, the lines, even the need to write linearly. Fill the page with messy, expressive, out-of-control handwriting. With chaos for a mother and imagination for a father, neat and tidy doesn't run in creativity's family.) ❧

*See Guideline 5 — Don't Worry about the Rules*

*The writer's first affinity is not to a loyalty, a tradition, a morality, a religion, but to life itself, and to its representation in language.*

— Jayne Anne Phillips

November 13   Remember an afternoon.
November 14   "The window had other views."
              (after Wislawa Szymborska)
November 15   Write about what's obvious.

## Discover What You Want to Write About

When I ask students in my writing classes what they want to write about, I often get big, broad answers like, "I want to write about my life in the military" or "I want to write about my crazy family." Or, they answer with wide-spreading generalities like "the relationship of mothers and daughters" or "the sixties."

*I never know when I sit down, just what I am going to write. I make no plan; it just comes, and I don't know where it comes from.*

— D. H. Lawrence

Whoever said "it's better to write about God's hat than God," was suggesting that rather than tackling expansive subjects that have no beginning, middle, or end, it's better to narrow your subject down to some specifics. Specific incidents, times, relationships. When my student Steve wrote about the time his character lost the company's bulldog mascot, he was writing about life in the military. Jodi, another student, wrote about the Thanksgiving dinner when Uncle Hendrick wore Aunt Lilly's chemise under his blue-striped shirt and Aunt Lilly choked on the giblets. This created immediate and specific examples of a crazy family. These details are the place to start.

To find out what you want to write about, try this:

On a clean sheet of paper, begin a sentence with "I want to write about … " Before your brain has a chance to kick in, grab a corner of the first image that comes to you and pin it down in a few sentences. Include specifics of time, place, people, and some sensory details. As soon as you have completed your paragraph (no more than four or five sentences), begin the next "I want to write about … " and once again, nab the image and begin writing it. Repeat this exercise until you've filled your page. Don't stop to think between paragraphs and avoid generalities.

If none of your images relate in any way to what you thought you wanted to write about, you may consider this a message from your intuitive self to your thinking self. Maybe you thought writing about The History of Women sounded more important than writing about the relationship between your mother and her sisters. But what is The History of Women except an eternity of specific relationships?

To keep your "I want to write abouts" within a particular subject and help focus your paragraphs, write a headline across the top of your page — Family Stories — and limit your listings to that subject area. Once again, don't stop to think of what you want to write; simply begin the paragraph with "I want to write about …". The directive of the headline and your intention will help focus your writing. Note: If images that don't relate to your subject continue to appear, pay attention and be willing to listen to your inner writer.

I'm a great believer in lists. Lists are a kind of mental shorthand, a fast way to get control of things. Lists can also help you find out what you want to write about. In her book *Journal to the Self*, psychotherapist and journal teacher Kathleen Adams taught me the value of making lists of 100.

Briefly, here's how to do it: Number your page from 1 to 100, then, as quickly as you can and without thinking (just like writing practice), make a list of 100 things you want to write about. Use single words or short phrases only, no details. Don't worry about repetition; repeated entries emphasize a topic's importance to you. Just get it down. Try making lists of 100 Memories, 100 Intriguing Situations, 100 Questions I Want Answers To, 100 Mysteries.

A surefire way to discover what you want to write is by uncovering what you have already written about. Within your notebook is a Hansel and Gretel trail of images, phrases, and words that appear and reappear. When you reread your notebooks, follow these bread crumbs through the forest of your writing. They will lead you home. 🐌

*See Images That Haunt You, Rereading Your Practice Pages, Create Your Own Writing Topics*

> *You write about what you know or you write about what you want to know.*
>
> — Jill Ciment

---

November 16    Write about the last night of _____.
November 17    Write of something done in a small moment.
November 18    These were the reasons to stay.
November 19    Write about being lost along the way.

## Tell Your Secrets

Revealing secrets is one of the dangers of being a writer. By laying yourself open to the page or whoever reads it you chance exposure every time you write. Even baring yourself to yourself can be frightening. "Being a poet is a damned dangerous business," said poet Carl Sandburg. But if you don't write your secrets, if you tiptoe nervously around whatever you've got concealed, you risk writing that is vague and untrustworthy. Also, holding back some things means being guarded about other things. The sentinel at your palace door is going to ask "who goes there" of every thought that might be cloaked in danger or intrigue. Woe be to the writer whose palace guard is paranoid and every thought suspect.

Divulging secrets, whether to yourself in your notebook, to your writing group, or to an even bigger audience, might be an experience you want to work up to. Here are some suggestions.

■ Write a secret on a blank page, then tear it up or burn it. The act of getting it out and on paper takes much of the power out of confidences. Write as many pages as you have secrets. Build a bonfire if you need to. (You don't have to do this all in one sitting; take as many sessions as you need. Do it each time you remember another secret.)

■ In a writing group, have each member anonymously write a secret on a slip of paper. Fold them up, drop them in a basket, and invite each person to draw one to use as a writing prompt. If someone gets her own secret, it could be the Muse saying now's the time to write about it. If that doesn't feel right, have everyone return the secrets to the basket and redraw.

■ Give your confidences to a fictional character (make her smart and beautiful and very rich) and let her tell them.

■ Ease into "that which you can never tell" like a stripteaser doing his or her act, revealing just a little at a time, first a wrist, then a shoulder. Stop when you feel you've gone far enough.

*See Take Risks, How to Tell When the Censor Is Present, Avoiding the Truth*

*You're told time and again when you're young to write about what you know, and what do you know better than your own secrets?*

— Raymond Carver

# Gifts of the Night — How to Use Your Dreams

Images that appear in the night can find their way into your writing. Dreams can solve problems and answer questions, invite the opening of a door, the looking out a window or into a room. Characters appear with messages and meanings. Your dream life can influence your writing life and your creative work can alter your dreams. And sometimes not even you can say what it all means. How do you use your dreams in your writing life?

*All writing is dreaming.*

*— Jorge Luis Borges*

■ Keep a dream notebook. Write your dreams when you first awaken; try to capture the details and sketch the images. Then make use of the surreal, non-sensical, imaginative, and surprising imagery of the dreams in your writing.

■ Keep paper and pen beside your bed to write down dreams that awaken you in the night. You may think you will remember them the next morning, but chances are you won't. Even the most powerful dreams can be as elusive as gossamer in the light of day.

■ Many believe you can ask for a dream. If you're at a stuck place or need a solution to a problem in your writing, ask the dream maker to bring you answers in the night. Invite your characters in, too.

■ Give your dreams to your characters. If you have a recurring dream of day-lilies breaking through the snow, loons flying overhead, or water seeping into your house, let your characters use the dream. Consider what the dreams might mean to the characters and how they might interpret them.

■ Use dreams as a starting place for a practice session. Begin with "I dreamed …" and complete the exercise as you would the "I remember …" exercise. You may be surprised at the dreams you recall using this technique.

*See The Writing Life — Writers on Dreaming*

November 20   Write about the booth in the corner.
November 21   Returning takes too long.
November 22   Write about a hesitation.
November 23   Write about being underwater.

## Breathe

Breathing is the link between our body and our mind. Sometimes we are so out of our bodies, we forget to breathe. Conscious breathing and then writing to our breath will connect us.

If the piece you're writing carries great emotion, or if you are frightened by what you're writing, you may forget to breathe. Your body becomes tense, the emotion builds, and fear grows until the tension is so great the only way to relieve it is to stop writing.

You put the pen down, close your notebook, and get up from your desk. The tension is relieved, but the piece you were writing, with its intensity and raw honesty, is lost, maybe gone forever.

Try this.

As you are writing and you sense the tension building, breathe into the feeling and continue writing. This can cause emotions to release and you may begin crying. If this happens, just keep breathing and keep your pen moving. Or, you may experience anger that you were trying to hold back by holding your breath. Breathe into the feeling and write the anger; write as big and bold as you need, press the pen into the page even to the point of tearing. Soon you will pass through to the other side of the emotion and calmness will return. Breathing has allowed you to experience the feeling and writing has enabled you to express it.

At other times, it may not be the heightened emotions that cause you to stop breathing, but the incredible energy of the piece you are writing. You get pulled into its intensity and not only forget to breathe, but grip your pen so tightly you experience muscle cramps. Again, breathe into the writing and relax your hold on your pen but don't stop writing. Breathing will help you keep your balance as you ride the crest of the wave until, finally, its energy dissipates and you roll safely to shore.

"Breathing, we bring our body and mind back together and become whole again," said spiritual teacher Thich Nhat Hanh. Breathing carries oxygen to the brain, grounds us physically, and provides a rhythm for our work.

Writing is a holistic act. To be completely present, use your mind, your body, and your soul. Breathing is the cord that binds all three together.

*With good writing, I think, the most profound response is finally a sigh, or a gasp, or holy silence.*

— Tim O'Brien

## When Can I Quit My Day Job and Be a Full-Time Writer?

Expecting to earn a living as a writer may be expecting too much. Especially for beginners. The fact is, only a small percentage of all writers in the United States earn enough money from their writing to support themselves. Many writers who've sold three, four, or five books still have to work at other jobs. And the payment for short stories is often in contributor's copies of the publication. "I thought that I would always have to have a day job and write in the evening," said Canadian poet and novelist Margaret Atwood.

The hard reality is, as a writer, you may be facing years of fitting your writing into a schedule that includes working a full- or part-time job. Add to that a family, friends, other responsibilities, and the romantic version of the writer's life that includes big advances; acres of time; a spacious, book-lined study; interviews; and book signings — that version of the writer's life wavers and disappears like a mirage on a long and lonesome blacktop highway.

If you've determined you want writing to have preeminence in your life, some reconstruction may be in order. Maybe change jobs to make more time for writing, even though it might mean less income. You may have to simplify; move to a smaller, less expensive place; make choices between vacations and writing; entertainment and writing; sometimes friends and family and writing. Sleep and writing. Will it be worth it? "People say poets can't make a living. I tell them to lower their expectations to match their income," said poet Nikki Giovanni.

If you expect to write and get rich, you will probably be disappointed. Rich

*You're a writer and that's something better than being a millionaire — because it's something holy.*

— Harlan Ellison

| November 24 | Write about opening a gift. |
| November 25 | Write about the fault line. |
| November 26 | This is what was left when he was gone. |
| November 27 | Write about a sudden storm. |

writers are as rare as ostriches in Alaska. On the other hand, if you write because this is how you are made and, like Raymond Carver who took refuge in
the car with a pad on his knee or novelist Sara Lewis who shut herself in the
laundry room at 4:30 in the morning, you write because you can't *not* write, it is
simply what you do, and whether or not it's worth it is a moot point; if you're this
kind of writer, there is no other way.

But for another kind of writer, the one who is not driven by a passion that
gives no sway, and who accepts the reality that he or she may never be self-
supporting through their writing efforts, and who will always have to make choices
between writing and something else, will it be worth it?

This is what Rainer Maria Rilke wrote: "Ask yourself in the quietest hour of
your night: must I write? Dig down into yourself for the deep answer. And if this
should be in the affirmative, if you may meet this solemn question with a strong
and simple, I must, then build your life according to this necessity." ✺

Beyond Practice

## A Field Trip to the Library

What better ingredient for your writing than the sacrosanct dust of a library. It's a virtual literary surround-sound, a place of order and generosity within an aromatic maze that is more than wood and paper and ink and glue and dust and time gone by. "My library was dukedom large enough," Prospero avowed in *The Tempest*.

For this Beyond Practice session, take your notebook on a field trip to your local library. (Remember the first time you entered a library?) Meander the stacks and gather books that call out to you. Fiction, poetry, art and photography, nonfiction, biographies, essays, books on time and place and history, compendiums, compilations, anthologies, collections. Children's books, cookbooks, science and technology books. Any book and every book that whispers *read me, read me*. Carry your armload of treasures to some quiet table and build a fort of books around you. Take your time and open one book at random; let the Muse choose the page. Savor the words as you read them, gaze into images, allow colors and shapes to amaze you. Let them inspire you to write.

Follow images that lead you into writing, or use phrases, sentences, or lines of poetry as prompts. Read, then write, then read again, allow a rhythm to arise from the taking in and giving out. Impression and expression. Impose a specific amount of time for each or let the natural flow that emerges be your guide. Remind yourself that there is no hurry. Just because you've selected fourteen books doesn't mean you have to look inside every one or use something from each for a writing prompt. Trust that the right book is the one in your hands, find what it has to tell you, then move to the next. If you don't get to all the

November 28   One Saturday night, …
November 29   Write about avenues of escape.
November 30   A woman named _____.

books you've chosen, know that there will be another time, another library day, another Beyond Practice session. And if your library card is current, you can always check out an armload of books to take home.

The best part: so long as we are active, vocal, and passionate users, supporters, and promoters of our public libraries, they will be there with their amazing abundance of books available for all of us.

Suggested topics, though you'll hardly need them:

- Write about bodies of water.
- Write about something that belongs to someone else.
- This is what woke me up.
- It was before …
- It was postmarked Pocatello.

# DECEMBER

"In the end, the best thing a writer
can do for his society is to write
as well as he can."

—Gabriel García Márquez

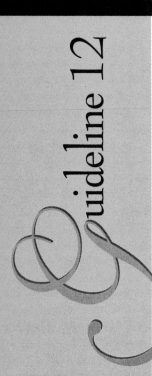

## Date Your Page and Write the Topic at the Top

Dating your page helps keep you grounded in the present while your writing soars into distant galaxies and travels through time. Noting the date will also give an order to your entries and can be used for gathering information: When was the first time Julio, that slippery character with topaz eyes and dangerous hands, appeared? When did I start writing the loaf of bread story? Is there some kind of synchronicity with my literary glimpses of the Moon and the actual moon cycles? What is the rhythm of my writing? Are there specific days when I write with ease and passion and other times when it's like swimming upriver after spring thaw? All these questions and more, dates on your page will readily answer.

By writing the topic at the top of the page you'll be able to reference pieces you might want to use in something else. You can also see how your mind works, the intricate weave of associations and connections. Also, in review, you may be able to tell which types of prompts are most evocative for you, which are least. Some writers work best from that which is solid and concrete — write about a used car you owned, you hear church bells in the distance; others respond better to abstract or vague phrases or images — under the surface of ordinary things, aftershocks of the full moon. This is good to know as you create your own topics or look to those ideas that will stretch you.

## How to Start a Writing-Practice Group

Writing in a group is an evocative experience for many writers. Some say they write better, take more risks, have more fun, and actually write more than when they write alone. And, almost to a person, they say they learn about writing from the group experience even if there's no actual feedback or critique in the sessions.

Groups can offer support, structure, and variety to the writing-practice experience. And there are those who believe the Muse likes to work crowds.

Meet in cafés, bookstores, or private homes, or in rooms in community centers, libraries, or schools; all you need is a place where you can stay a while, where you won't be distracted during the writing time, and where you can read aloud after you've completed the writing.

To start a writing-practice group, you can begin with just one other person. Set up a time and a place, bring notebooks and topics (or make them up when you get together), and go to it. Take turns offering topics and keeping time.

To attract more participants, put notices on bulletin boards in cafés, in community newspapers; put the word out at bookstores and on the Internet. The larger the group, the longer the meeting time must be, so that everyone can have an opportunity to read. Let the group determine how long the sessions should be and how frequently to meet. Use the guidelines on page 8; you may even want to read them at the beginning of each session.

Happy writing.

See *Find Your Tribe — Why Hang Out with Other Writers, Find Support for Your Writing Life*

*I write to understand as much as to be understood. Literature is an act of conscience. It is up to us to rebuild with memories, with ruins, and with moments of grace.*

— Elie Wiesel

---

### Writing Topics

December 1    Write about an invitation refused.
December 2    ... and nobody objected.
December 3    I recall that evening together.
December 4    Write about an unforeseen friendship.

## How Writing Heals

When you write about that which gives rise to pain from the deep place of memory and body where it resides, you literally feel the emotions that surround it. Tears often accompany bringing these feelings to the page. By writing it, you acknowledge the pain and its cause. Acknowledgment is the first step in recovery. When you read your work aloud you give voice to your feelings. These are some of the ways writing heals.

It is an act of courage to complete such writing. Edging toward the pain may feel like nearing the perimeter of a great black hole. This is how it felt when I tried to write about my husband's death. For years I was able to write only fragments, the feathery wing of memory, a muted image. Finally, after a decade, I sketched the skeleton of a story, thin and pale as his body during those final months. The story remains incomplete. But still, each time I work on it, I continue to heal from the loss.

Amy Tan said, "In the telling of stories something happens, your whole perception and memory of things begins to change and you can let go of what you have just told — you give it away." In letting go, we heal.

Think of how we tell stories when catastrophe strikes. Or when marriages go asunder or relationships end, after injuries or accidents or violence we experience or witness. Again and again we relate the tale. We're on the phone or writing letters or e-mailing. We stand on street corners, stop mid-aisle in grocery stores; we meet in restaurants, cafés, and bars and say to one another, "This is what happened." It is the nature of humans to recount events, to give way to feelings.

Writing them down helps us accept our experiences and emotions as real — after all, there they are in black and white. Acceptance is another step in recovery.

More than just a way to express our feelings, writing lets us feel them; it leads us into the deep places of our heart and shines a light so we can bring these stories from inside to outside. This movement creates some space, perhaps just enough to feel our heart beat or take a breath, but enough to let us know we are still alive.

When we hear or read others' stories, we bear witness to their experience, which is healing for them and for us. Through our written and spoken voices we connect in ways that reassure us we are not alone. Realizing that others have the same hungers and longings as we do, that their fears, bewilderment, and pain are the same as ours, allows us to experience our commonality. Only then can we feel compassion. Love follows compassion's footprints and, surely, the healing of great wounds cannot be far beyond this.

In his book *Poetic Medicine, The Healing Art of Poem-Making,* poetry-therapist and teacher John Fox wrote, "Poetry is a natural medicine; it is like a homeopathic tincture derived from the stuff of life itself — *your experience.*" He said, "Poetry provides guidance, revealing what you did not know you knew before you wrote or read the poem." The same can be said for other types of writing you may do: journaling, free-writing, stream of consciousness — the kinds of writing that emerge when you become unselfconscious and write from that deeper place, the heart place.

Stories that ache to be told are your psyche's way of longing to be healed. Painful though it may be, listen to these urges, take courage, and write them. 🐦

*See Being Vulnerable on the Page, When Your Writing Embarrasses You*

*The role of the writer is not to say what all can say but what we are unable to say.*

— Anaïs Nin

| December 5 | Write about a series of mishaps. |
| December 6 | This is what she said. |
| December 7 | Write about hard times. |
| December 8 | Write about winter constellations. |

## Dance with Your Shadows

As we write, we stumble into hidden recesses of ourselves, those places under the eaves where shadows sway in half-light and croon our names. A seductive tango, raucous rock and roll, a ballet of treachery, writing plays the tune and the writer dances. We may insist that we don't know the steps, but we do, we do.

Our shadowy self is that part of us we find unacceptable. This is what psychoanalyst C. G. Jung told us. Somewhere before our second decade we shut her down, put him away, denied and repressed that part of ourselves. The part that grew up to be a tango dancer who wears slinky black dresses and a rose in her hair that is so unlike our cotton skirts and Birkenstocks. Or that rock and roller who jumps and shouts and parties all night long when the "real" us is all business suits and Bach.

But shadows don't go away; they follow behind us, matching our every step with their own. Turn quickly and they disappear. Or they spread before us, lurching large and misshapen on the pavement beneath our feet. They come out and dance by the light of the Moon.

There's more, too. Where do we find these characters who are capable of stealing babies and trashing hotel rooms, who lie and cheat and set cars on fire? Imagination yes, and perhaps shadowy urges best left to fiction.

Susan Wooldridge wrote, "To become more fully who we are, it's a good idea to invite our shadow to speak now and then." Give him a few hours and listen to what he can tell you. You'll learn your own secrets and get a different perspective. ("Oh, so that's what it feels like to sleep in until noon." "Flirt with younger men? *Certainement.*")

Dance with your shadow, I say. Welcome her with a cup of tea and a sweet cake if that's what pleases her or a beer and a smoke, whatever potion or poison will lure her to your table. Roll back the rug, clear away the furniture, and follow your shadow's lead. Then head for your notebook and get it all down while your body still moves to the rhythm she set.

*If you want to write you have to be willing to be disturbed.*

— Kate Green

## Writing Goals

Setting goals is a way to accomplish specific projects and create a discipline for your writing. Some writers use a word count, others a page count, still others, a set amount of time to write every day. Remember Upton Sinclair's ambitious 8,000 words a day? Japanese writer Yukio Mishima wrote from midnight to dawn and Louisa May Alcott wrote *Little Women* at the rate of a chapter a day.

Work with different goals to find the method that serves you best. Above all, be realistic. If you set your goals too high and can't accomplish them, you may find yourself so discouraged that you give up doing any work at all. Disaster! On the other hand, if you're not stretching, you're not growing as a writer. And open ends have a way of never closing.

Let's say over a period of a few weeks of regular writing practice, you discover that during a fifteen-minute session, you write about 400 words. You could set a goal of 500 words a day, and push yourself another few minutes, with a goal of 2,500 words of raw, first-draft writing each week (writing five days a week). Or make a goal to practice six days a week, or every day. Or stretch your writing time to an hour, which probably would not equate to 1,600 words a day. (Even the bounteous Anthony Trollope could only maintain 250 words a quarter hour.)

My friend Greg set a goal of working from 9 A.M. to 2 P.M. five days a week. Notice I said working, not writing. During that five hours he writes first-draft material in his notebook, edits what he has written in previous days, rewrites stories he's presented in his read-and-critique group, and studies the craft through reading books and journals about writing. He also has his favorite double mocha (no whip, nonfat) and spends some time observing.

*You aim for what you want and if you don't get it, you don't get it, but if you don't aim, you don't get anything.*

— Francine Prose

| | |
|---|---|
| December 9 | Behind lace curtains. |
| December 10 | Write about seeing someone for the last time. |
| December 11 | Write about a late night phone call. |
| December 12 | I carried it in my pocket. |

Another way of setting goals is to participate in a read-and-critique group that has a fixed number of pages you can submit per session. Maybe eight or ten manuscript pages (double-spaced, wide margins, about 250 words per page) each time. This quota could be your goal. Bear in mind, manuscript pages are not the raw stuff of writing practice. This is work you have rewritten and shaped — material from your notebook distilled and revised into something more polished.

Once you know your speed and tempo, you can set other goals: four short stories completed and submitted this year, first draft of a novel by December, six finished poems this spring. Goal setting is another expression of your commitment to your writing. ❧

*See The Writing Life — Quotas and Other Facts and Figures, Daily Routine, The Discipline of Writing*

*Without pressure, the work doesn't get done at all.*

— William
　Saroyan

## Writers on Why They Write

**Marcel Proust** wrote, "this life that at every moment we distort can be restored to its true pristine shape … within the confines of a book."

**Isabel Allende** sees writing as an act of hope, a communion with our fellow man.

**Umberto Eco** said he is continuously trying to find the meaning of things under the text.

**John Keats** wrote for the "mere yearning and fondness" he had for the beautiful. To him, it mattered not if "my night's labors should be burnt every morning and no eye shine upon them."

When asked by a student why she wrote, **Eudora Welty** said, "because I'm good at it."

**Mary Gaitskill** called stories the "right, unseen underlayer of the most ordinary moments." She said she got great satisfaction from plunging her hands into that underlayer.

**Michael Ondaatje** believes writing links up one's own life with the history of our time.

**Richard Ford** likes the notion that literature is a gift from the writer to the reader.

**Will Carlton** said his purpose in writing is "to touch and draw out that vein of poetry and feeling which exists somewhere in every human nature."

| | |
|---|---|
| December 13 | This is the difference between men and women. |
| December 14 | Write about a street you lived on. |
| December 15 | Write about a red convertible. |
| December 16 | "I walked into the Maverick Bar in Farmington, N.M." (after Gary Snyder) |

# Create Your Own Writing Topics

It's not that some people don't know what they want to write about, in fact, there is so much they care about, they can become paralyzed by the infinite choice of subjects. Everything is right and nothing is right.

Here are some ideas to help you create your own practice topics.

■ Write the words "I remember … " at the top of a blank page then, without hesitation, write the next words that come to you. Be specific. Write some of the details of what you want to write about, not just the idea of it.

"I remember walking that path beside the Adriatic in Cevat, when it was still Yugoslavia, the gray rocks as big as moving trucks and the piney deep green scent of the trees. I remember being homesick.

"I remember drinking cherry cokes with single, long-stemmed maraschino cherries. The marble-topped back booth at Kruger's Drug Store where Betty Barnes and Sharon Mallory and I giggled and blushed and told boy stories.

"I remember driving the road that climbs the mountains behind Santa Barbara the day before Christmas. The morning was crisp as toast with a sky that held blue like it was the one true thing. All around me the hills yawned and stretched and above, a hawk landed on a telephone line and eyed me as I cruised by."

As soon as you've completed a few sentences of the image, and before you stop to think of the next, drop down a few lines and begin again with the words "I remember … " and write the next snapshot that comes. Do it again and again until you've filled a page. Each of these "I remembers" becomes a door into a writing session.

■ Stash notepads and pens in all your reading locations (I've got them beside my bed, near my little nook in the kitchen, tucked in the cushions of the couch, on my desk, in the car). When you come upon a phrase or image that strikes you, write it down. Do this with everything you read — novels, short stories, nonfiction, poetry, newspapers, magazines, and cereal boxes. Once taken out of context, the phrases and images assume a random quality entirely separate from their source. Store these slips of paper in a file folder or envelope that you can dip into on your way to a practice session.

■ Go within the belly of your own writing for topics. Here you'll find images

*I find that I actually have to write in order to discover my ideas. I think you could allow yourself to never get started if you tried to guess in advance what was going to inspire you.*

— Jay McInerney

and phrases of your own making that can also be used outside of their original context, just as those of other writers.

■ As others read aloud from their writing, make notes of phrases that resonate with you. You may want to let your writing friends know you are using their material as a prompt. Not all writers take kindly to such borrowing, while others consider it a compliment.

■ Use song lyrics as writing prompts. Try to stay away from the familiar, which would be akin to using a cliché for a topic, and go toward the lesser known.

■ Every day for a month, create a first sentence in your writer's notebook. Don't worry about how or when it might get used or the identity of some character whose name appears in one (or more) of the sentences. After you have a month's worth of these starters, cut them into strips, fold them up, and put them in an envelope. Wait a while until you've all but forgotten what you've written before you begin pulling these for writing topics. Spontaneity is always a good ingredient for a practice session.

On the bookshelf in my writing space is a tiny red satin box filled with words to use as writing prompts. A pale woven straw box with a lid contains strips of sentence stems, folded and waiting; a rotund basket spills over with my postcard collection. Envelopes stuffed with writing topics are secreted between books; a shallow wooden bowl holds clippings from a book of poems. On the shelf next to a round-faced clock leans a tall red loose-leaf notebook, its pages lined with topics from past practice sessions, to be used again or not. Create your own library of writing-practice prompts. You'll never be at a loss of what to write about. ☙

*See Discover What You Want to Write About, Rereading Your Practice Pages*

*Surprise is where creativity comes in.*

— Ray Bradbury

| | |
|---|---|
| December 17 | Write about a redheaded woman. |
| December 18 | Write about masks. |
| December 19 | You are in a church. |
| December 20 | Write what you didn't say. |

# Work Schedule, 1932–1933 — Henry Miller Miscellanea

## COMMANDMENTS

1. Work on one thing at a time until finished.
2. Start no more new books, add no more new material to "Black Spring."
3. Don't be nervous. Work calmly, joyously, recklessly on whatever is in hand.
4. Work according to Program and not according to mood. Stop at appointed time!
5. When you can't *create* you can *work*.
6. Cement a little every day, rather than add new fertilizers.
7. Keep human! See people, go places, drink if you feel like it.
8. Don't be a drought-horse! Work with pleasure only.
9. Discard the Program when you feel like it — but go back to it the next day. *Concentrate. Narrow down. Exclude.*
10. Forget the books you want to write. Think only of the book you *are* writing.
11. Write first and always. Painting, music, friends, cinema, all these come afterwards.

## DAILY PROGRAM

**Mornings:**
    If groggy, type notes and allocate, as stimulus.
    If in fine fettle, write.

**Afternoons:**
    Work on section in hand, following plan of section scrupulously. No intrusion, no diversions. Write to finish one section at a time, for good and all.

**Evenings:**
    See friends. Read in cafés.
    Explore unfamiliar sections — on foot if wet, on bicycle, if dry.
    Write, if in mood, but only on Minor program.
    Paint if empty or tired.
    Make Notes. Make Charts, Plans. Make corrections of MS.

    *Note*: Allow sufficient time during daylight to make an occasional visit to museums or an occasional sketch or an occasional bike ride. Sketch in cafés and trains and streets. Cut the movies! Library for references once a week.

# Find Support for Your Writing Life

Whether it's in the DNA or a dowry that's doled out by the gods — you be a painter, you a musician, you a chef, you a teacher, you a writer — or perhaps something more random or even more holy, the gift of writing isn't given to everyone. Choosing a writing life means honoring that gift, and sets you a little or a lot outside the norm and makes you a part of a world others might find different, odd, foreign. Because the writing life does go outside the lines, family, coworkers and bosses, and certain friends may not be the best source of support for writers. Yet support is what all artists need. Here's a list of people and places to find encouragement, assistance, and friends along the way, and why writers need this.

*It's hard to conceive of yourself as a writer, so you await proof before you take that plunge and say, "I'm a writer."*

*— Diane Johnson*

■ Writing friends. Especially one or maybe two best writing buddies to whom you can talk about your writing and your writing life. This is the place to bring your doubts and fears, your insecurities, admit your flaws and foibles. These are also the people with whom you discuss ideas, work through writing problems (life problems, too). You can even boast some with these friends; they'll applaud your successes and cheer you on. And you'll do the same for them.

■ Writing groups. This is where you go for critique of your work. To listen to others' ideas, writers whose opinions you trust and whose work you respect. Writing groups meet regularly, monthly at least, often weekly, and are made up of a core group that offers continuity and ongoingness, people who are familiar with your work and you as a writer.

■ Classes, workshops, and seminars. This is a place for learning about the craft from writers whose work you admire. Here is where you'll find teachers and

| December 21 | Write about a scar. |
| December 22 | It's Sunday morning. The phone rings. |
| December 23 | Write about something you want but cannot have. |
| December 24 | Write about a fire. |

mentors and others who can broaden and deepen your writing world.

■ Conferences. You learn about the craft at conferences; participants often have the opportunity to meet and interact with editors and agents as well.

■ Readings and book signings. Here's a chance to hear authors read their own work and to meet and chat with writers you might otherwise never meet.

■ Internet. Everything from on-line chats to Q & As to guest appearances by authors. Plus opportunities to publish your work, take classes, and hook up with writers across the country and around the world. On-line writers' groups are formed and reformed, appear and disappear only to appear again. You'll find listings of all things writerly from events to books on writing, publications, and more. Keyword: writing. ❧

*See Find Your Tribe — Why Hang Out with Other Writers, How to Start a Writing-Practice Group*

## It's All Copy

Writers live life on two levels: one where we participate in relationships, go about our daily business, interact, respond, and perform; the other in which we observe and take notes. We can't help it. It's in our writer's bones. Part and parcel of being a writer.

There's a story of the time author and screenwriter Nora Ephron's mother was in the hospital. "Take notes," the older woman urged from her deathbed, "it's all copy."

Everything we observe, all that we are part of, all our feelings, thoughts, reflections, and prayers, the aggregate of all that happens, goes into the stew pot from which we ladle our work. No need to feel you have nothing to write about; you have everything. "There are significant moments in everyone's day that can make literature," said Raymond Carver. "That's what you ought to write about."

For example, you're writing a play and your character is holding her baby. You remember the time you held your own child against your breast, that she weighed less than a bag of potatoes. You pause in your writing, form your arms around a phantom baby, and remember your infant in that warm nest, the faint drumming of her heart against your own. You remember the sweet roundness of her cheek and how her lips bowed together, wet and pink. When you lean down to take in her scent, those long-ago feelings of love and protection rise on the intake of your breath. It is from within this real-life scene stored away in your writer's memory that you resume your writing.

All of your life is such grist for the mill.

There are times it may feel immoral or even exploitive to take such notes. Like the mother-writer in Lorrie Moore's award-winning story "People Like

*If one writes about oneself, the real motive must be, I think, to give reassurances to other people.*

— Christopher Isherwood

| | |
|---|---|
| December 25 | "We ate Chinese." |
| December 26 | Write about something sacred. |
| December 27 | Write about a time someone told you a secret. |
| December 28 | If I tell you the truth … |

That Are the Only People There," when their baby had been diagnosed with cancer and the husband said, "Take notes. We are going to need the money." "No. I can't," she said. "Not this! I write fiction. This isn't fiction." Or the time my own father was dying and I sat beside him on the edge of one of those cold vinyl-covered chairs hospitals provide. I didn't want to notice his ropy hands wrapped around the aluminum bars of his bed, willed myself to not look at the color of his toenails, blue as a bruise under the awful fluorescent lights. But my experience was like Lorrie Moore's character's, who at the end of the story said, "Here are the notes."

So even as you kiss your lover and lean against his naked chest, you make note of the curve of his neck as it gives way to shoulder, the muscles in his back; even as you watch in terror as your three-year-old tumbles from the jungle gym, you observe the way her tiny body free-falls through space and the look of disbelief in her eyes. These are the notes and scratches with which you fill your notebooks, like a squirrel storing for winter, nuts of experience and observation that will feed your writing. Fair warning to such lovers, family, friends, and acquaintances — you're a writer and it's *all* grist for your writing mill. ❧

See *Transferring Real Life to Fiction, Writing about Real People, Truth versus Fact*

*The world is made up of stories, not atoms.*

— Muriel Rukeyser

## Writing Retreats

To retreat is to withdraw, and for writers this means withdrawing from the daily world to a place where your writer-self is nurtured and cared for. You can retreat at home by closing yourself off from outside disturbances, disconnecting the phone and remaining in solitude, or go elsewhere, to a friend's cabin in the woods, a bed-and-breakfast in the next town, a retreat center across the country.

Retreats can last for half a day, half a month, or half a year. Dian retreats for a twenty-four-hour period of every week, Sandy goes away for one month every twelve, Roger has been in Spain for more than a year. For this Beyond Practice writing retreat, include at least one overnight so you can breathe deeply and refill yourself, give time to simply being. Invite one or two writing friends if you like, more if the space allows, or go alone if solitude is more appealing. The idea of retreat is to rest, summon quiet, and replenish.

For the past few years, several writer friends and I have created retreats together. This is how our retreats are structured, more or less: The first day is a time of arriving; each person brings simple food to share, books and journals, music perhaps, notebooks, and maybe a manuscript to read aloud. After dinner, a brief writing session may be scheduled, just for warming up and setting out intentions. More often than not, the evening will be spent allowing our bodies to rest and our souls to transition.

Next morning, each awakes as she will; there is no schedule — some will share breakfast, others begin with a walk and journal writing. A writing session begins at nine. Working from words or phrases each offers on tiny slips of paper piled in the center of the table, we do five-, ten-, fifteen-, ten-, and five-minute

| | |
|---|---|
| December 29 | These are the delicacies of a ruined evening. |
| December 30 | A random light. |
| December 31 | In anticipation of the night. |

writes, reading after each writing. After the morning session, some plan activities together, some go solo; after lunch together, another writing session is scheduled for half past two and, following that, the afternoon is free until dinner together in the evening. After dinner, someone reads a manuscript. The evening drifts until all find their beds. The next day is more of the same, and so on.

Follow this outline, or be even less structured, and let the writing come as it will. You may want to bring specific projects to work on, but also take long walks, gaze out windows, eat leisurely and simply. Leave your watch at home and let your body tell you when to eat, when to sleep, when to move, and when to be still. Light candles, build a fire, watch the rain. Attune to the sensory.

Here are some topics to take along.

- Write about promises broken.
- Write about the last light of day.
- Write about a secret collection.
- Write what whispers your name in the night.
- Notes drawn from the river.
- Write about a whole life of madness.
- This is where I've been.

*Nothing you will do will make a difference if you can't face the solitude.*

— Tom Robbins

"I write. The longer I live, the more convinced I've become that I cultivate my truest self in this one way."
— Tom Chiarella

# Recommended Reading

There are so many great books on writing, creating this short list was like choosing an ice cream at Ben & Jerry's, an exercise filled with indecision followed by regret for what I didn't select. This list includes books about writing in general — the attitude and philosophy of writing, rather than instructions on the craft. But there are dozens of really good books about the craft, too. After you've finished these, I urge you to visit your library or your bookstore and browse the stacks.

Aronie, Nancy Slonim. *Writing from the Heart, Tapping the Power of Your Inner Voice.* New York: Hyperion, 1998.

Bradbury, Ray. *Zen and the Art of Writing.* New York: Bantam Books, 1992.

Brande, Dorothea. *Becoming a Writer.213* 1934. Reprint, Los Angeles: J. P. Tarcher, 1981.

Browne, Rita Mae. *Starting from Scratch, A Different Kind of Writers' Manual.* New York: Bantam Books, 1988.

Cameron, Julia. *The Artist's Way: A Spiritual Path to Higher Creativity.* Los Angeles: J. P. Tarcher, 1992.

Dillard, Annie. *The Writing Life.* New York: Harper and Row, 1989.

Epel, Naomi. *The Observation Deck, A Tool Kit for Writers.* San Francisco: Chronicle Books, 1998.

Gardner, John. *The Art of Fiction, Notes on Craft for Young Writers.* New York: Vintage Books, 1991.

Goldberg, Natalie. *Wild Mind, Living the Writer's Life.* New York: Bantam Books, 1990.

_____. *Writing Down the Bones: Freeing the Writer Within.* Boston and London: Shambala, 1986.

Lamott, Anne. *Bird by Bird, Some Instructions on Writing and Life.* New York: Pantheon Books, 1994.

Ueland, Brenda. *If You Want to Write.* St. Paul, Minn.: Gray Wolf Press, 1987.

Welty, Eudora. *One Writer's Beginnings.* Boston: Harvard University Press, 1984.

Wooldridge, Susan G. *Poemcrazy, Freeing Your Life with Words.* New York: Clarkson Potter, 1996.

S. E. SHELLCLIFFE

## About the Author

Judy Reeves teaches writing and leads creative writing workshops. Among other books, she is editor of the *Brown Bag Anthology*, a collection of writings originating in her writing-practice groups, which continue to meet twice-weekly after six years. As a member of the Second Story Writers, a women's writing ensemble, two of her plays have been produced. In 1993, she cofounded The Writing Center, a nonprofit literary arts organization. She lives in San Diego and is at work on her first novel.

New World Library is dedicated to publishing books and
cassettes that inspire and challenge us to improve the quality of our
lives and our world. Our books and cassettes are available at bookstores
everywhere. For a complete catalog, contact:

New World Library
14 Pamaron Way
Novato, California 94949
Phone: (415) 884-2100
Fax: (415) 884-2199

Or call toll free: (800) 972-6657
Catalog requests: Ext. 50
Ordering: Ext. 52

E-mail: escort@nwlib.com
http://www.nwlib.com